MW01244311

Above All Others
and other Prairie Parables

David Johnson

By David G. Johnson
Sketches by John S. Wilson

Printed in the United States of America
PINE HILL PRESS
4000 West 57th Street
Sioux Falls, S.D. 57106

Dedication

To First Lutheran Church of Sioux Falls

When I retired from the parish ministry in 1999 I thought my parish activities were concluded. I sold or gave away boxes of books, thinking I would pursue other interests. But, after a brief interim stint at East Side Lutheran in Sioux Falls, I joined the staff at First Lutheran in August of 2000. I have been there ever since, now on a part time basis.

First Lutheran is a large congregation with a warm heart. For example, one Sunday I mentioned from the pulpit that I was going to ride in the MS (Multiple Sclerosis) 150 mile bike ride. I asked if they could help me out with a few dollars of sponsorship money.

By the time I climbed on my bike for the two-day ride, I had over $2,900 in sponsorship support from the members of First Lutheran. I was overwhelmed by such generosity. Yet, it was typical of the caring spirit which prevails in the congregation.

I have been fortunate over the years to serve in congregations that allowed me to be myself. No attempt was ever made to fit me into some kind of pre-conceived pastoral mold. Part of the reason for that kind of freedom, for me and others, at First Lutheran is the way in which grace is highlighted and practiced.

With new and impressive facilities and a desire to become "A Welcoming Home in the Heart of Sioux Falls," First Lutheran will continue to be a beacon to those who are seeking a home where God's love touches each heart. I have found it a good place to call "home."

Table of Contents

Above All Others 1

God's House. 5

The Journey 9

The Blacksmith 13

A Book. 16

The Parade. 20

Change. 24

Political 28

Maintenance. 33

The Christmas Program 38

Looking Back. 41

The Falls 45

Pioneers 49

The Light House 53

Gossip 57

Determination 62

Music. 66

Choices 71

Jesus. 75

Rest 80

Bells 85

Unlocked 89

Grace 93

Foreword

Years ago as a student at Augustana College in Sioux Falls I took a course on Shakespeare from Novelist in Residence, Herbert Krause. Professor Krause would come to class laden with piles of his favorite books, from which he read during the class. As we sat with our Shakespeare text opened before us, he would sprinkle his lecture with all sorts of personal observations and interpretations. Some of us jokingly declared we learned more about Krause than we did about Shakespeare. But that was neither a fair nor accurate assessment. Instead, we sat in the presence of a teacher who let Shakespeare flow into life through him. The course could have been called "Krause meets Shakespeare." However unorthodox Krause's methods may have been, they were certainly effective. He brought Shakespeare to life through a variety of stories, anecdotes and other supplementary material, lifting the English bard off the pages of the text into the middle of life. I, for one, was never tempted to skip the class.

There was a stretch in my life when I avidly collected old wooden duck decoys. As with any collecting interest, there was more to it than meets the eye. One naturally deals with the many facets of decoy making, various histories of wildfowling, important carvers and stylistic features from different areas of the country. The hobby facilitated a convergence of several of my interests—history, wildlife and folk art. I gradually accumulated a shelf full of books on decoys. Of all the books I read on the subject the most interesting and memorable were the personal stories from authors who recalled how they had come to find the decoys. They recounted a variety of experiences—with old time market hunters who had shot over the "blocks," or climbing into the dusty lofts of long neglected sheds, or finding a prize specimen at a flea market or sometimes the often protracted negotiations required to buy the "birds." They wove into the stories their own thoughts, surprises, ecstasies, disappointments and hopes, as well as providing valuable information for evaluating and identifying the great variety of decoys. Often I felt as though I had been there with the author. Usually I felt as though I would like to have been there—first.

I have just finished reading Harvey Cox's new book, *When Jesus Came to Harvard.* Cox wrote the book out of his experience as the teacher of a course at Harvard College called "Jesus and the Moral Life." In his book Cox delves into the content of the course, but he also describes in some detail his own thoughts about the subject as well as the response of his students. It is an arresting approach to theological and moral subjects. I found myself interacting with the themes as though I was in the classroom.

Meanings emerge from the stories. Not only does Cox convey the insights of his course through story, he also highlights the importance of stories for humans. He mentions various ways in which we are similar to animals. We stand erect, but so do gorillas. We know that we will die, but possibly elephants do too. We communicate with language, but dolphins seem to speak to one another in clicks and groans. But, Cox asks, is there any other creature that tells stories?

The thread that runs through Shakespeare, as taught by Herbert Krause, the collecting of old decoys and Harvey Cox's account of his class at Harvard is one of personal story. Many of us do not belong to churches where personal testimonies are encouraged. But, as we do more with small groups, Bible or book studies for example, we discover the inevitability and even desirability of what we might call "testimony," the sharing of thoughts, anecdotes from our past, new discoveries and convictions.

It is in that spirit that I continue to push on with my Prairie Parables. Our stories can often highlight for others various themes of "His Story." When Christian themes are woven into the fabric of our own stories they take on colors and textures that are striking. We can see and feel the thoughts better.

I am deeply grateful to my friend, John Wilson, for his delightful sketches. I never tell John what to draw as a heading for each chapter. He reads the chapter and decides for himself. I am always pleasantly delighted by his imagination as well as his artistic talent. Since winning the federal duck stamp competition he has remained active and busy as an artist but he is always willing to help a friend.

My daughter, Kari Mahowald, has provided some much needed help in reviewing the manuscripts. Her attention to detail is greater than mine and her suggestions have made the book more readable. Having had a mother and now a daughter as English teachers has at least helped me see the importance of grammatical correctness, even though I have not always accomplished it.

Finally, I want to thank the folks at Pine Hill Press. With an eye to both economy and attractiveness, they are committed to helping local authors publish.

—Dave Johnson

Above All Others

My hometown of Oldham has a water tower now. It's not a recent addition, but it is an improvement made since I left town. Dray trucks used to deliver our water to our cisterns, one load at a time. When there was a fire the dray truck would deliver water to the fire truck, gradually losing ground to the fire as it returned to the city well for another load. To the outsider approaching the town by car the most noticeable difference is the skyline. Oldham's skyline used to be defined by the two grain elevators standing next to the railroad on the east side of town. Now the small but attractive water tower looms over the city and the elevators.

Oldham is typical of most prairie towns. Long before you see any evidence of a population center you see the water towers rising from the horizon as you travel the highways of South Dakota. Should you wander off the beaten track on to the maze of gravel and dirt roads following the section lines you might welcome the sight of a water tower, much as a ship tossed at sea in a storm welcomes the beam from a lighthouse. More than once I have been guided to my destination by the sight of a gleaming silver water tower on the distant horizon.

There has not been much poetry written about water towers but that does not mean they are without poetic content. Consider what each community is saying to the rest of the world when it erects a water tower.

With the building of a water tower each community is admitting dependence. The unspoken admission is this: "We who live here are a community of people totally dependent on water, and we prefer that the water be quickly available to us." Water is the life source of any community. Nobody thinks it's a sign of weakness to admit this need for water. No community has ever, out of some sort of silly pride, tried to camouflage the water tower so others would not notice it. Water is so essential to life that we have no hesitation in declaring our primal need to everyone who approaches us.

Water towers are also a way by which a community identifies itself. I can't recall ever seeing a small town water tower without the name of the community boldly painted on it. One assumes that everyone living in the town knows what town it is so the painted name must be there for the benefit of visitors and strangers. On the other hand, it never hurts for those who live within the tower's shadow to be reminded that they are a part of a community where, likely, the whole is greater than the sum of its parts. Hometown pride, rather than neutrality or shame, fueled the desire to have the name—big and bold—up there high in the sky for all to see. After all, it is no small thing to live within and be a part of a community.

Isn't that about the same kind of dynamic we experience when we raise the cross above our Christian community? Some of us may actually belong to a congregation where the cross towers above the church building. And if the outward design is less classical, the cross will certainly be granted a prominent and elevated position in the sanctuary. Even without the physical sign of the cross those who live within the Christian community are always aware of living under the shadow of the cross. Some who regularly make the sign of the cross on their bodies find it to be a helpful way to stimulate that awareness.

Just as when a small town erects a water tower over itself, Christians also readily admit their dependence by raising a cross over themselves. God took a dreadful instrument of the cruelest kind of death and turned it into a glorious instrument of life and hope. When we live beneath the cross of Jesus a radiance streams into our lives, replacing a dry, cotton-mouthed attempt at some sort of self-concocted spirituality or filling a cavernous emptiness. The apostle Paul gave eloquent testimony to the centrality of the cross in the lives of Christians. He told the Corinthians that when he came to live among them he did not want to make the kind of splash that would call attention to himself. His one thought was to point to the cross of Jesus, so "that it might not be emptied of its power." (I Corinthians 1:17) To raise the cross over our heads is to readily admit, even proclaim, our most basic need to drink the water of life. It is a declaration of dependence on Jesus.

The cross also declares who we are, as boldly as a town's name on a water tower. A World War II chaplain spoke to one of our classes when I was in the seminary. He recalled an incident in New Guinea. He had just arrived with other troops when a native of the country rushed up to him and pointed to the cross on his lapel, shouting "Me Jesus man too."

The hymn, "Lift High the Cross," speaks of the magnetism of the cross. It draws people to itself. There are folks who wonder who Christians are and we say, "Don't look at us but look up to Jesus." There are folks out there on the gravel and dirt roads of life, often confused, sometimes lost. We hope they will see the cross. We hope we are raising it high enough. We hope it will draw them to Jesus.

Nobody outgrows the need to stand at the foot of the cross and to look up into the face of Jesus. It is where we take our stand in order not to forget who we are. I am not thinking now of the flagrant sinner so much as those of us who frequently speak of Jesus. At the foot of the cross we fall silent and listen. All good deeds, all well crafted sermons, all eloquent prayers dissolve in silence. Now is the time to listen, to be absorbed in his presence, to trust that he has conquered all, to receive his love. It is the place where we are most apt to utter the words that cause the angels to break into song, "My Lord, I love you."

Water towers dot the prairie landscape. They call our attention to a community of people—people who are boldly admitting their total dependence on the water that flows into their homes, schools and businesses. They remind us of how important it is to be aware of sources. Communities cannot subsist without that great supply of life-giving water that fills the cavernous tank above them. Nor can we who are spiritual beings ignore God's ample supply of grace.

And the towers are beacon-like too. Some of us are prone to take the back roads—to see new country. We can lose our bearings. "Now where do I go," we mutter. Then we spot the dot on the horizon and know. From there on we are drawn. Likewise, in one form or another, the cross is to be raised high enough above the normal landscape of life for all who are searching to see. "If I be lifted up," said Jesus, "I will draw all to myself."

Even for those who live within the town the water tower is a steady reminder of who they are. They know, of course, but it is all too human to drift into a kind of solitary confinement and forget the larger community. We are encouraged, as we look up, to ask what it means to be a part of this town. What does it mean to say, "This is where I am from, this is my home." Christians, too, look up to Jesus and find that in him they have found a home. Jesus is the one, above all others, to whom we belong.

God's House

Four of the five congregations I have served during my years in parish ministry have built new facilities recently—East Side Lutheran, Peace Lutheran, First Lutheran, all in Sioux Falls, and Lutheran Church of Our Redeemer in Watertown. All of these congregations are very dear to my heart. Each has had or will have a Service of Dedication. What does it mean to dedicate a new church building? I pass some thoughts about this on to these congregations as a kind of forgotten, but still perky, voice from their past. Maybe it is even a kind of love letter. Perhaps some scattered ruminations about church dedications can be applied more generally.

When President Abraham Lincoln traveled to Gettysburg on November 19, 1863, he was invited to make a few appropriate remarks in order to "set apart" the grounds of the National Soldiers' Cemetery for its sacred use. He delivered ten sentences in less than three minutes. In what is known to all of us as the *Gettysburg Address* he said, "It is altogether fitting and proper that we should do this." "But," he continued, "in a larger sense, we cannot dedicate, we cannot consecrate, we cannot hallow, this ground. The brave men, living and dead, who struggled here, have consecrated it, far above our power to add or to detract." The dedication of the National Soldiers' Cemetery would instead be a part of a process to begin on that day. The actions of the nation rather than the words of one person would carry the most dedicatory power, said Lincoln. "It is for us, the living, rather, to be dedicated, here, to the unfinished work that they have thus far so nobly carried on," Lincoln observed. He called for a national resolve to insure "that these dead shall not have died in vain."

Any dedication encompasses both a past and a future. The present moment, the moment of Dedication, is a time to sense and appreciate the energy of the past as well as future challenges.

A church looks back on the road it has traveled. Its history, its traditions, its stories come into a sharper focus. One remembers a particularly gifted lay leader who shared a vision. One recalls a special person who held everyone's feet to the fire on the subject of missions. One thinks of those who shared their skills—sewing quilts, baking pies, teaching Sunday School, pruning trees, planning events, organizing libraries or singing and ringing and playing instruments to make adoration joyful. Many who have been sacrificially generous remain nameless and if their identity was revealed it would be a huge surprise to everyone.

And, of course, one remembers the family that could not worship unless they were always sitting in the same pew, a heavy burden to bear in a day and age when there are no pew rentals. And the lady who persisted in referring to the candelabras as "candle-a-bras." And the fellow who was so confident the pastor would not make a mistake that he always fell sound asleep during the first five minutes of the sermon. And the card who first introduced himself to the new pastor by saying, "I'm a Norwegian and a Lutheran and a Christian," causing the pastor to ask, "In that order of importance?" And the parishioner who sometimes complimented one of the pastors on a fine sermon, when it was the other pastor who had preached. Ah, there are many stories, some humorous, some touching, some tragic, but all memorable and a part of the spiritual fabric of a congregation, all played out and retold against the background of the cross.

The long look backwards is ultimately directed to the cross of Jesus. That event marks the beginning of each congregation. Just as Lincoln credited the brave soldiers of the Civil War with having already consecrated the hallowed soil of Gettysburg so we too must say that this place, this building, has already been consecrated by the bloody sacrifice of Jesus. We simply acknowledge and offer thanks for our Lord's dedication to his mission and to us. We thank Jesus for stirring others to plant the cross in this place. We praise the Master for including us in his blueprint.

A Service of Dedication also looks to the future. Solomon, son of David, was the third of the three great Kings of Israel. It fell on his shoulders to build a great temple and fulfill a dream of his father, David. In his prayer of dedication Solomon acknowledged that God was much larger than the temple being dedicated. Solomon prayed, "But will God indeed dwell on the earth? Even heaven and the highest heaven cannot contain you, much less this house that I have built?" (I Kings 8:27) God's name would dwell there and people would have a place to which they could direct their prayers, but God would be out and about, accomplishing his purposes.

In some respects Solomon saw the temple much as we would see a brand new army training camp. It might be a stunning project, a state of the art installation. But it is not an end in itself. Soldiers do not go to a training camp and stay until they retire. Rather, the army trains and equips them for battle and then moves them out, to fight for their country and defeat, confound or contain the enemy. So the temple was to be a staging ground to prepare people for the struggles of life and to help the children walk before their God, even as their ancestors had.

There is something about the dedication of a church that turns the tables on us. It calls for a dedication of ourselves too. The dedicatory event, even though it is all about the new facility, has a way of pulling us into the heart of the church's life. How shallow to gather and dedicate a place where God's glory will be celebrated, if we do not intend to gladly be among the celebrants.

The poet, Edwin Markham, wrote about the building of cities. But what he said could easily be transferred to the building of churches.

> "We are all blind until we see
> That in the human plan,
> Nothing is worth the making
> If it does not make the man.
>
> Why build these cities glorious,
> If man unbuilded goes?
> In vain we build the building,
> Unless the builder also grows."

Or one could say, "Why build these churches glorious, if man (or woman, or children) unbuilded goes? It may be initially difficult when a congregation has invested several million into a new facility to think of it as being strictly utilitarian and thus meant to be worn out. But that is the idea behind any church dedication. The focus is on how people will benefit from new opportunities for worship and fellowship and how their serving God and neighbor will be enhanced. The building has grown up from the ground in order that the builders may now grow in their faith, hope and love.

What a joyous day it is for a congregation to gather together to give thanks to God for a new building and to dedicate it to the glory of God! Maybe it was only a handful of folks who had the initial dream. Maybe there were some who initially drug their feet. Perhaps others still feel it was a bit too extravagant. A few may think even more should have been accomplished. But now those memories and thoughts take a back seat to the joy and gratitude the congregation feels. The day has arrived for the dedication. It is a day full of grace and a day of response. Those who dedicate the building also dedicate themselves to God's glory.

The Journey

The journey of a lifetime for me consisted of a train ride from Oldham to Lake Preston. I suppose I should add that it was the journey of a lifetime up to that point in my early years. There would be other memorable journeys of somewhat greater consequence to come. But at the age of ten this topped anything yet.

The Oldham Dragons were playing the Hayti Redbirds in a basketball tournament in the afternoon bracket. A couple of my friends and I prevailed on our folks to let us take the train to Lake Preston. The passenger train was part of the Milwaukee Railroad but we referred to it as either the "Galloping Goose" or "Leaping Lena." It came up from Sioux Falls and arrived in Oldham about noon. Then it continued on up north, turned around at Bristol and came back through Oldham at night. Both the passenger train and the freight train gave us sense of being connected to distant places.

Lake Preston was not a destination of great distance. It was only eleven miles north. But when we boarded the train the sense of adventure would have been no less had we been leaving for Europe. My father brought us down to the depot, bought our tickets from the stationmaster and passed us on to the conductor when the train arrived. As the train left town we felt a kind of independence quite new to us. We were on our own, ten going on twenty-one.

Knowing that my father was, at that moment, also heading north to Lake Preston in his car so that he could meet us at the train depot took little away from the moment. Instead, I think it added to our sense of freedom because it was a freedom couched in the kind of security we needed at that age. It was comfortable to feel that we were on our own. It would not have been comfortable to actually be on our own.

We were far too intimidated by the enormity of the adventure to cause any trouble. But, if we had been of that mind once we put a few miles between my father and us, it would have been a sobering thought to realize that in a few more miles we would meet him again. It was a journey bracketed by my father.

I have often reflected on how that little train ride is a parable on life as a whole. Life is a journey from the cradle to the grave. Those of us who have achieved three score and ten years may have a bit more awareness of how journey-like life is than those who are in their early years. We certainly are more acutely aware of the swiftness of the journey as we look back and wonder where the years have gone. And, if there is a heightened inclination to be reflective in our senior years, we may be more aware of God's guiding hand. God's presence always seems to be clearer in retrospect than in prospect.

The prophet, Isaiah, spoke of God's role in our beginning of life's journey: "Thus says the Lord who made you, who formed you in the womb and will help you." (Isaiah 44:2) Taking the Genesis account of God's creation of the world, Isaiah put it into personal language. All of life is a miraculous gift, including you and me. As each embryo takes form in the womb God takes notice and declares a love and faithfulness to that one soon to be born.

In the Old Testament book of Deuteronomy, Moses addressed the people whom he had led out of Egypt and through the desert for forty years. He was near death and not optimistic about either their desire or ability to remain faithful to the God who had brought them to the threshold of the Promised Land. In what is called "The Song of Moses," Moses used the past tense to hint at future problems. "He (Jacob) abandoned God who made him." (Deuteronomy 32:15). Moses pursued the theme: "You were unmindful of the Rock that bore you; you forgot the God who gave you birth." (Deuteronomy 32:18) Forgetfulness of their origin, Moses reasoned, would become their most serious problem and the results would be devastating.

I can recall when my father scolded me over the same issue, though on a much lower level. I needed a screwdriver for some little task and grabbed the first tool I found on my father's workbench. Unfortunately it was a quarter inch wood chisel. You can imagine what happened to the sharp edge of the chisel when I used it for a screwdriver. My father provided a convincing lesson on the importance of using tools for purposes the manufacturer intended. To use them otherwise was harmful to the tool. Moreover the chisel did not work all that efficiently as a screwdriver.

Scripture makes the same point. God created us for certain purposes and not for others. The Bible can be viewed as an owner's manual, containing the manufacturer's instructions on how the product was made and for what purpose. It also includes instructions for maintaining and repairing the product. To forget the manufacturer's purpose and instructions is to invite disaster. The author of Psalm 8 did not forget.

> "When I look at your heavens,
>   the work of your
>   fingers,
>
> the moon and the stars
>   that you have
>   established;
>
> what are human beings that
>   you are mindful of
>   them,
>
> mortals that you care for
>   them?
>
> Yet you have made them a
>   little lower than God,
>
> and crowned them with
>   glory and honor." (Psalm 8: 3-5)

The author of Psalm 8 carried his head high because he saw himself as a living, breathing miracle. This was not a status achieved through human effort, but one granted by our creator. As the saying goes, "think highly of yourself, God doesn't make junk." Our God formed us; it makes sense to let God form our lives too.

Our journey of life may be long or short, in human terms, but like all journeys it will come to an end. There is a destination to this journey. God will be there at the station to meet us when we step off the train. Is that a promise or a threat?

There is a hint of threat to this truth, picked up especially in the theme of the last judgment. Scripture provides an inescapable summons to responsibility and accountability. Would we want it otherwise? It is an indication that God takes us seriously.

One of the most difficult adjustments I faced when starting my ministry was the lack of evaluation. I had gone to school for twenty years and during all of that time my work was graded. I took pride in doing well. Good grades and teachers' affirmations goaded me to strive for excellence. Then, all of a sudden, I found myself in a rural, southern Colorado community as pastor of a small church comprised mostly of farmers and ranchers. On Sunday morning I preached a sermon, we sang a hymn and everybody went home. These were not effusive folks, bubbling over with compliments or, for that matter, with criticisms. Feedback was in short supply and not until I converted myself into a kind of judge of myself did I find a way out of what seemed to be a limbo of indifference. By the way, I think the evaluations were there; they were just not verbalized, at least to me.

God will be there to meet us at the end of our journey. Hopefully we will be able to present ourselves as persons who have not frittered away the gift of life. But most of all we will welcome the opportunity to be embraced by Jesus who will say of us, "this one is very imperfect, his journey has had its ups and downs, but he is a believer, saved not by his goodness but by grace." What a welcome!

The Blacksmith

As youngsters in Oldham, my friends and I would sometimes wander in to John Groce's blacksmith shop. The shop had its own peculiar odor and was always a little smoky. It was a place where things happened. John might be found welding broken machinery for farmers anxious to get back out into their fields. Or he might actually be making a new part, which was as close to manufacturing as it got in Oldham.

When he had to make a new part John would fire up the coals with his bellows. After the coals were thoroughly heated John laid a rod or band of iron into the coals and left it there until it glowed orange. Then with a mighty hammer or other tools designed to provide leverage he would cut or shape the metal to suit his purpose. John was an artist, employing his experience and imagination to make the right cuts and bends in the metal. He had no templates and each task required original thinking and some degree of experimentation. The artistry of many of the early blacksmiths has never been adequately noted, but they were creators as well as fixers. Their art was utilitarian rather than decorative—bordering on folk art. Although in recent years I have known a couple of blacksmiths who have created some wonderful metal sculptures. The demand for their services has lessened in recent times.

The Bible presents a similar picture of God. God, like a blacksmith, fixes and shapes his people, often allowing them to be softened by the fires of life so that he can bring into being a new shape.

As an adult, the seventeenth century English poet, John Milton, went blind. One can only assume it was a devastating blow, especially for the greatest scholar among the English poets. In 1637, three years after going blind, Milton spoke of his burden in the sonnet, "On His Blindness."

> When I consider how my light is spent
> Ere half my days, in this dark world and wide,
> And that one talent which is death to hide
> Lodged with me useless, though my soul more bent
> To serve therewith my Maker, and present
> My true account, lest he returning chide;
> "Doth God exact day-labor, light denied?"
> I fondly ask. But Patience, to prevent
> That murmur, soon replies, "God doth not need
> Either man's work or his own gifts. Who best
> Bear his mild yoke, they serve him best. His state
> Is kingly; thousands at his bidding speed,
> And post o'er land and ocean without rest;
> They also serve who only stand and wait."

Yes, he spoke of his burden but he also alluded to its result. His soul was "more bent" to serve his Maker. Milton allowed himself to be bent rather than choosing to react bitterly. When life deals us a heavy hand we may have to confront the options Milton faced. Will we be bent or bitter? Bitterness causes one to become brittle, to the point of breaking. But being bent means God can make us more serviceable.

At the age of 14 I went to work for uncle Milton on his farm west of Garretson. I had not grown up on a farm so operating any kind of machinery was new to me. He put me on the Farmall "H" and sent me to one of his fields to cultivate corn, with a minimum of instruction. There had once been a farmstead in the middle of the field but all that remained of it were a few trees. Milton had planted corn around the trees; for him they were not an impediment to either planting or cultivating. But, in following the row adjacent to the trees, I did not turn fast enough and I hit one of them with the cultivator, bending one side of the cultivator badly. In that position the blades would have sliced through the field, barely making a mark. Milton was a remarkably patient man, and he quietly took the cultivator off the tractor and headed for the blacksmith in Garretson. When he returned the cultivator was as good as new, bent back to its original shape, even though it was a little blacker on the side where the heat had been applied to make it malleable to the blacksmith's purpose. And that day, I became a better tractor driver.

The Apostle Paul discovered how God works when we are weakened by harsh experiences. Paul speaks of how he was given a "thorn in the flesh." Scholars have wondered if Paul was partially blind or experienced a form of epilepsy, due to the fact that he dictated his letters. The torment he experienced over his affliction was like a blow from Satan, he said. He prayed three times to be released from this scourge but the answer he received was not what he had hoped for. It was better. "My grace is sufficient for you," said the Lord, "for power is made perfect in weakness." As the blacksmith is able to apply his power to the metal weakened by the fire, so God is able to have a greater impact on us when we have been weakened by life. Paul concluded, "Whenever I am weak, then I am strong." (II Corinthians 12: 7-10)

Of course we do not have to wait for calamity to hit us before we acknowledge our weakness or our readiness to trust God. I have been in the ordained ministry for forty-four years and have served Holy Communion to many people. So many hands have reached out for the bread and taken the cup. Some of those hands have been thick and strong—hands of farmers and laborers. They take the delicate wafer and guide it to their mouths and testify to their longing for a strength beyond their own.

In his book, *The Wounded Healer*, Henri Nouwen speaks about the blessings latent in loneliness, a general human condition if there ever was one. The wound of loneliness, he says, is like the Grand Canyon—an incision in the surface of our life which can become a great source of beauty and self-understanding. He goes on to say that the Christian life does not relieve us of loneliness but blesses and protects it as a precious gift. Might we say that loneliness, as well as many other problems of life, softens us and allows our Heavenly Father to shape us into servants, bending our souls to love one another. That would be a gift.

A Book

My mother was an English major at Augustana College and later taught English at several South Dakota high schools—Astoria, Oldham and Big Stone City. She also taught at home. I can't think of my mother without recalling how concerned she was that I use the right grammar. It was her conviction that there was a right way and a wrong way to speak or write our language and one might as well do it the right way. She respected our language and she respected me enough to go to the trouble of correcting me when necessary, which was quite often. I found it mildly irritating at the time but appreciate it now. I'm afraid I have carried on the "tradition" and my children and a few others (whom I really had no right to correct) might grumble a bit and think of me as being finicky over the fundamentals of grammar. That is not to say that I am always correct in my usage of English. Knowing that, I continue to be grateful to those who think enough of me to offer suggestions or corrections. I view it as a form of friendship.

Mother's major effort with me focused on reading. She was an avid reader and wanted me to pick up the habit. I did, but at first it left her uneasy. I was a voracious reader of comic books. Mother worried that I might get lazy as a reader and stick to whatever offered pictures along with the text. Comic books, she felt, were frivolous and produced lazy habits. She probably feared that I would grow into my thirties without saying anything more profound than "Shazam."

Not to fear mother. I love to read and want to offer a testimony to the joy of books.

Actually it was mother, in her own devious way, who got me started reading books. She introduced me to the Sugar Creek Gang mystery books written by Paul Hutchens. Published by Wm. B. Eerdmans Publishing Company, they had Christian overtones. I read all of them with great fascination, including *The Sugar Creek Gang Goes Camping*. A sampling:

> "I'd never been actually lost in my life, but I began to feel like it, and it's a crazy feeling. Any direction you happen to look is either north or south or east or west, if you think it is, which it isn't. That's how you feel when you are lost." (*The Sugar Creek Gang Goes Camping*, p. 42)

If we came across a Sugar Creek Gang book I did not have, while shopping in Madison or Brookings, mother would open her purse without hesitation if I asked her to buy it for me. Her purse remained closed in the face of most other pleas.

Her passion for reading spread forwards and backwards. Her father and my grandfather, Chris, confined his reading to three newspapers, *The Garretson News*, *The Daily Argus Leader* and a Norwegian paper, *The Decorah Posten*. Grandma added the love stories in McCall's magazine to her reading list. Somewhere Chris had picked up the directive that if I ever wanted a book I should be helped to get it.

When I accompanied him to town as he delivered cream and eggs and picked up the necessary supplies, he gave me a nickel for treats. Sometimes my grandmother would rifle through his pockets before we went to town and slip me an extra nickel or dime. I remember wandering in to the Drug Store in Garretson in quest of an ice cream bar and spotting a 207-page book called *Touchdown To Victory* by Charles Lawton. I still have it and see by the inside cover that the price was sixty cents, 12 times the usual allotment. But when I asked my grandfather to buy it for me he did so with no questions asked. It may be that my willingness to forfeit the ice cream treat carried the day. Later that summer he also bought me a companion volume, *Home Run Hennessey*, by the same author. Since I was alone with my grandparents there were plenty of quiet places and spaces for reading. Hence, some would say, began my slovenly habit of hiding between the pages of a book when there was real work to be done. I loved those books. They took me into worlds far beyond the little farm west of Garretson.

I'm afraid I took a bit of a furlough from reading during my high school years, though I do recall getting caught up in Whittaker Chamber's book, *Witness*, and a few others. Sports and a developing interest in girls pushed the books to the side. But the professors at Augustana College had their own unique way of reminding me that books are good and one should spend some time with them. They not only demanded that I read books but also remember what they were about. The professors at Luther Seminary were as unrelenting in their persistence that books were the key to education as were the professors at Augustana. Not surprisingly my professors at the University of Kansas Graduate School continued to steer me to books, some of which they had written.

Since leaving formal education I have never been tempted to not read. I think I can boil my reasons for continued reading down to three points, and I am immodest enough to pass them along.

First, reading stimulates creative thought. This may be a slight overstatement, but as a preacher one has to learn to tell the same story 52 different ways. Writing sermons is a very daunting task. One strives to be faithful to the basic message and creative in telling and applying it. Of course, it is wonderful to find illustrations in the material one reads. But even if that doesn't happen I find that reading helps to keep the creative juices going. The dry spells I have experienced over the years can usually be traced to a delinquency in reading. Reading a good book keeps the mental wheels turning.

Preferences in reading will vary. I love biography and other historical subjects. And I find it almost impossible to put down a Jon Hassler or John Grisham novel. I have friends whose reading tastes lean towards mysteries. Maybe it doesn't matter much so long as a person lives with a book for a while.

Second, I read for information. Someone once said a sermon should be prepared with a Bible in one hand and a newspaper in the other. I agree to a point. But I think that other hand ought to hold books on preaching, Biblical studies, pastoral care and systematic treatments too. Even if one does not pursue an organized curriculum of continuing education one can lay out a personal program of reading within ones own vocation. Those of us in parish ministry are generalists, and we have much to learn from the specialists even though we will never master any of the fields as well as they.

Third, I read just for the sheer enjoyment of it all. I have never had much desire to learn speed reading. I prefer to read more slowly and savor the words and the way in which a good writer puts the words together. I think I can safely say that I have always preferred the book rather than the movie when I have read and seen both. It is such a great treat to sit down with a good book—well worth the price of the book, considering the cost of other kinds of entertainment.

As I wind up this little chapter I am temporarily diverted as I gaze at my two six foot shelves full of books. I have read most of the books and forgotten more than I remember. I think of all the work and learning that has gone in to writing those books. How many years of research and study are represented on those shelves? The answer would be overwhelming. Each of those books has fed me along the path of life. They are old friends and deserve the kind of respect we show to those who have made a difference in our lives. And, like most old friends, maybe they deserve to be looked up from time to time.

The Parade

This chapter requires a brief introduction. I have become known in local circles for telling stories about my hometown of Oldham. Until now and from now on, all the stories have been and will be true. But recently I was invited to present a report from Oldham in much the same way as Garrison Keillor recalls the news from Lake Wobegon on his radio broadcast, "A Prairie Home Companion." That invitation carried with it some opportunities for fiction that were readily and with relish accepted.

It's been a quiet week in Oldham, my hometown.

They are still talking about the Potato Days held there last summer. For one thing, the parade was huge. This year there were 37 John Deere tractors entered in the parade. That beat the old record of 29 green tractors, set two years ago. The success of the parade is pretty much determined by the number of John Deere tractors. Most observers thought the parade was twice as long as any other year, but actually this was the first year the parade had gone around twice so it gave that appearance.

The float everyone talked about was the one that carried the ushering team from Oldham Lutheran Church and their newly won trophy. The ushers had raised enough money through bake sales and rummage sales to go to the National Lutheran Ushering Olympics in El Paso, Texas last spring. They entered two of the events and won them both, giving them the overall highest point total and with it a huge trophy.

The parade gave them a chance to show off their new purple and white uniforms. Oldham lost its high school a few years ago and many of the folks had been missing those moments of pride when the Oldham Dragons' basketball team took the floor in its purple and white uniforms. To restore some of that pride the ushers decided to purchase purple blazers and white slacks. They had Oldham Lutheran Church emblazoned on the backs of the blazers, but decided to leave the fire-breathing dragon off. There was already enough fire coming from the pulpit when pastor Enquist preached. They were a snappy group as they marched to the front of the church in step with "Holy, Holy, Holy."

As I said, they entered two events in the Ushering Olympics. One event was called "Gathering the Offering." Unlike most ushers who simply grab the offering plates and start passing them down the pew rows, the Oldham ushers believe the offering ought to be a time of serious pageantry. So the team splits into halves and goes up to the front of the church on each side aisle. Then they cross over to the other side of the church. As they meet in the center they do a nifty bit of sleight of hand as they trade plates, giving with the right hand and receiving with the left hand, much like two deep return football players exchanging the ball on a kickoff. The exercise is performed so quickly that those who are sitting in the back of the church don't notice. They continue back down the opposite side aisle and come to formation in the center aisle in back of the church, prepared to move up once the organist plays a few measures of what sounds suspiciously like a cavalry charge.

Part of the rationale for these unusual maneuvers was to make the offering a memorable experience for all the people. Then, too, by the time of the offering a number of people had been numbed by Pastor Enquist's sermon and needed to be reawakened. But maybe the real reason has a bit of a commercial ring to it. The ushers had noticed that when they received the offering in the old, more laid back way, the people who had forgotten their envelopes never had quite enough time to make out a quick check. About the time someone was writing in the amount on the check the plate would come streaking by faster than a Johan Santana fastball, or so it seemed, and there would be no offering from that person. Now those who forgot their envelopes have plenty of time to write out a check right there in the pew. The ushering team supplied a financial report to the Olympic judges showing how offerings had picked up since they inaugurated their new format.

The judges were impressed and gave them a rating of 10 for degree of difficulty and also a 10 for imagination.

The second event the ushers entered was "Seating People in the Front." For years they had fought a losing battle. An usher would spot someone waiting to be seated. He would show a bulletin but not give it out and then beckon the worshipper to follow him to the front of the church. But the desire of the ones being seated to avoid sitting in the front of the church was stronger than their desire for a bulletin and they would inevitably slip into one of the back pews. Meanwhile, the usher, thinking they were still following him, would parade all the way to the front, turn around and discover to his horror there was no one there. It was a humiliating moment for the usher and more than one of them experienced a loss of confidence and quit out of embarrassment.

Fred Peterson, one of the ushers, came up with a novel idea. He suggested they ought to seek training. So the whole team went out to Oscar Olson's sheep ranch to watch Oscar's sheep dogs work the sheep. The ushers observed how the dogs worked together, some behind the sheep and some off to the sides as they pushed the sheep forward to the open gate. Watching the dogs, the ushers came up with an idea. They, too, would work together, behind and to the side of the people. When people arrived at church two ushers would slip in behind them, give them a little push and move them forward. If the people showed signs of wanting to stray into a pew before reaching the front, one of the ushers would move up and block the way. All the while the ushers made muffled sounds of encouragement. Some thought it sounded a little like dogs barking. No, it was just a little, barely audible, rhyme they used: "To the front we go, fast or slow, to the front we go." The Olympic judges awarded them a 10 for style and a 10 for degree of difficulty.

They won both events and that was enough to give them the first prize, a beautiful trophy with an usher giving hand signals on the top. So far Pastor Enquist has resisted putting it on the altar, much to the disappointment of the ushers. But Pastor Enquist is fixed in his belief that it would not be appropriate to have anything, like that trophy, towering above the cross or, for that matter, blocking his view of the congregation and the ushers at work.

Lots of out-of-towners showed up for Potato Days to watch the parade. Many of them were strangers. Strangers are usually regarded with some suspicion in Oldham. One of them, on his way out of town, pulled up in front of the local tavern. Knute Hanson was sitting on a bench outside the tavern and the stranger yelled to him, "What's the quickest way to Sioux Falls?" Knute looked him over carefully and said, "Are ya drivin or walkin?" Somewhat impatiently the stranger shouted back, "I'm driving, of course." "Ya," said Knute, "Dat's da quickest way." Word of Knute's helpfulness got around and a few thought he ought to be designated as the head of a new Visitors' Bureau.

And that's the news from Oldham, the little town on the edge of Lake Thompson, where all the women are gorgeous, all the men are tough and all the children are way above normal.

Change

I don't remember who suggested I could do it. I believed that person. So it was with a great deal of self confidence that I launched my sales career. Actually it was to be a very limited career—a summer job. I signed up to sell a certain brand of aluminum cook ware. I went to the weekend training event held at a cabin in Minnesota. There the other recruits and I learned how to cook without using water. No boiling of anything was permitted. The theory behind this rule was that the heat spread so quickly and uniformly through the aluminum that the usual process of boiling vegetables in water was unnecessary. Unnecessary, yes, and ill advised too since boiling sucked the helpful minerals out of the vegetables.

We were trained there at that cabin to be missionaries for efficient cooking and healthy eating. We hoped for some serious financial gains too. Our trainers equipped each of us with a huge suitcase of assorted pots and pans and a sales talk. Then they turned us loose on the world. That's when the downward spiral began.

Every salesman needs a customer. I turned first to some old friends from my hometown of Oldham—a young couple who had married and moved to Sioux Falls to work. They were probably as poor as I. But my comfort level was more important to me than the prospect of clinching a sale. I told Maxine about the way one cooked vegetables without water. She was dubious.

Confidently, I suggested we run a little test. She could boil carrots in the usual way and I would cook them my way. She turned up the gas stove, put carrots in her kettle with water and carrots in mine without any water. I am still not sure what happened but it must have been that the flame was too high and more or less went right through the bottom of the pot because while her carrots boiled nicely in the bubbling water mine burned to a crisp. For the rest of my time there we sat and talked about old times in Oldham and ate Maxine's carrots. Topped with a little butter and pepper and salt, they were delicious. After she opened the windows the room gradually cleared of the smoke from the burned carrots.

I may have tried one or two other folks—either friends or family—but that was about it. My confidence was shattered. Moreover, my heart was not in it. Truth be told, I did not really care very much how people cooked their vegetables as long as they were happy with the method. They could have used an empty coffee can (with lots of water) for all I cared. And I think to be a successful sales person one has to believe mightily in one's product. The zeal for waterless cooking found no abiding place with me. I spent the rest of the summer, which was all of the summer with the exception of one week, wheeling concrete on a construction job. I had found my level of competence. I was happy.

Some may describe my summer pilgrimage as cowardice or lack of determination. I may have even entertained the notion that I was a failure. We have to deal with self-incrimination throughout our lives. It seems to come especially easy to those of us who are Norwegians. On the other hand, maybe there was an element of wisdom, even courage, in abandoning ship at the first hint of disaster and seeking a change in direction. Sometimes it's ok to admit we have hit a wall. Since that time I have come across the theory that each of us is in danger of realizing the so-called "Peter Principle," meaning that we often move up in life until we arrive at a point one level above our competence. I know the "Peter Principle" is true. I experienced it. And maybe my pots and pans debacle was not the last time I proved the principle to be true either.

Older people are usually singled out as the chief resistors of change. I'm not sure that is totally accurate. I recall when serving a South Dakota congregation how the youth were practically unanimous in their objection to change. When I served as a pastor at East Side Lutheran Church in Sioux Falls somebody floated the idea that maybe we ought to change the name of the church to reflect some Christian teaching rather than cling to a name that only gave our location. The suggested name change was "Lutheran Church of the Resurrection." A few of the older folks tossed the idea back and forth but the eighty youth in my confirmation class were solidly against any name change. They did not even want to talk about it. I think there was something threatening to them in the very idea of change. It may have seemed to them like a rejection of the past or that something they thought of as fixed and solid had suddenly become wobbly.

Change is neutral. Any comment on change almost always has to have a qualifier. It depends on what and why the change is suggested or happens. The American philosopher, Ralph Waldo Emerson, once said "a foolish consistency is the hobgoblin of little minds." As we grow in knowledge and wisdom it is likely we will change our minds from time to time. A friend of mine frequently prefaced his opinions with the phrase, "according to the light I now have." He left room for more light to be thrown on the topic and the possibility that he might change his thinking. Half the college professors in the world would quit if they thought all the freshmen were incapable of changing their minds as they learned and grew during the four years of exposure to new ideas and accumulated knowledge.

On the other hand change may be something to avoid. In the hymn "Abide With Me," we sing "Change and decay in all around I see; O thou who changest not, abide with me." That kind of change is more of a collapse of something good. When we describe someone as having changed it may be for the good, but it may also be a way of saying that someone has taken the wrong path and the change is regrettable. And we certainly lose our respect for someone who has no fixed position and is therefore constantly changing his mind. In a political campaign it is regarded as a black mark against a candidate if it can be shown he or she has shifted positions according to which way the winds of public opinion blow. Consistency is much to be desired. Who would want to vote for somebody who waffles on important issues?

Sometimes change is unavoidable and is a part of what we might call progress. Sometimes change is something we must do when we come up hard against the facts. In the long run it will be for the better. Sometimes change is devastating if we lose what is most important to our security and well being. Recovery may be slow. Change, in and of itself, is neither bad nor good.

With all of the relativism that accompanies the many kinds of changes with which we are confronted and which we must make or avoid, it is important to have one fixed and unchanging center. The author of Hebrews helps us find a changeless center: "Jesus Christ is the same, yesterday and today and forever." (Hebrews 13:8) Whether we have changed from selling cook ware to wheeling concrete, whether we have moved from the farm to town, whether we have shifted our allegiance from one political party to another, whether we have gone from good to bad, or visa versa, there is one who does not change.

He will strengthen your heart by grace. (Hebrews 13:9) Jesus will provide the strength to make the necessary changes, to avoid the objectionable ones and handle those that come on their own. We can count on that.

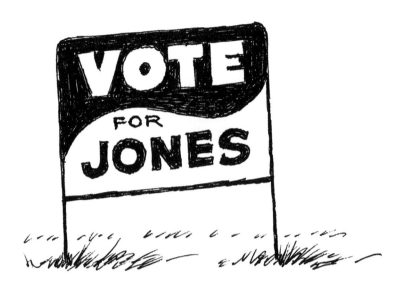

Political

Every couple of years we are subjected to political campaigns. When politics is in the air some regard it as a major form of air pollution while others breathe deeply and find it invigorating. Political parties and candidates spend an enormous amount of money these days to capture our vote. It doesn't take much imagination to think of ourselves as targets with politicians looking through their scopes at us. In spite of that, I believe a good word needs to be spoken for politics.

I recall when, in 1950, Sigurd Anderson ran for governor of South Dakota. He came to my home town of Oldham and my father, the Lutheran pastor, escorted him up one side of the main street and down the other, introducing him to business people and their customers. The separation of church and state was thus suspended, at least for one day. Sigurd Anderson was a charming person and a gifted campaigner. He had a down home way with people and an uncanny ability to remember names. Stories abound of how he ran into persons he had met only once, even years before, and greeted them by name. I was proud, through my father, to be associated with this good and important man. He won the election, much to my satisfaction.

Another earlier experience of a political nature had left me somewhat befuddled. We were visiting a farm home and Oscar, the host, and my father sat huddled over the radio listening to South Dakota's Republican senator Karl Mundt give a speech. The gentleman of the house was a rock solid Democrat who had no appreciation for Karl Mundt. The speech filtering through the speaker on the radio drew muffled but sharp expressions of disgust from Oscar, who disliked Mundt for his political persuasions and for having defeated Oscar's friend, Emil Loriks, in an earlier congressional election. I was shocked to hear this wonderful and jovial man so angry and bitter in his renunciations of our senator. I thought a United States Senator should be respected, not denounced.

Later, as a confirmation student, I learned that the fourth commandment had a political side to it. To honor one's father and mother meant not only to respect and obey our parents but also those who had any kind of authority over us, including teachers and policemen, governors and presidents. To this day I carry that frame of mind with me if I am in the presence of a mayor, governor, congressman, senator or president. I might not have voted for the person or agree with all of her or his positions or decisions, but I am respectful of the office—and the person, if at all possible.

The apostle Paul left us with a clear statement of our obligation as citizens of a country. In Romans 13 we read: "Let every person be subject to the governing authorities; for there is no authority except from God, and those authorities that exist have been instituted by God." Paul continued to elaborate: "For rulers are not a terror to good conduct, but to bad." Government is "God's servant for your good," Paul concluded. Keep in mind that Paul did not live in a democracy and yet he could still affirm the necessity for order and law enforcement in a peaceful society. God wants us to live in peace and harmony and calls us to seek justice. Following Paul's train of thought we learn that good government is ordained by God and those who construct and maintain the government (that is, those who are political) are God's servants. All who become involved in the political process, as campaigners, voters or office holders, are God's servants.

Martin Luther elaborated on Paul's words through his writing about the two kingdoms, the Kingdom of Christ and the Kingdom of the World. In the Kingdom of Christ God rules through the gospel, offering forgiveness and shaping hearts to be motivated by love. But in the Kingdom of the World God rules through the law where governments make rules and punish those who disobey. The Kingdom of the World encompasses everybody whereas the Kingdom of Christ includes only those who live by faith in Jesus. To attempt to govern a society only through the Kingdom of Christ would not take into account the pluralism of all jurisdictional units and the lack of perfection even on the part of believers. Thus, God ordains governments to provide safe and secure environments.

The word "political" derives from the Greek word "politicos," meaning "of a citizen." The first definition given by Webster is: "1. Of or concerned with government, the state, or politics." "Political" is ideally suited for usage in a democracy where citizens select and shape the government. There is not much that is political about a monarchy or dictatorship. Nor is it likely that one would use the word "political" in a condition of anarchy. "Political" is a word that suggest ordinary people are somehow the ones who hold the power and that the government is "of the people, by the people and for the people." (Abraham Lincoln)

So why do we sometimes find politics to be so distasteful? To answer that question I suppose we might come up with descriptive adjectives like "partisan," "negative," "self-serving," "corrupt" or "compromising." Politics always seems to be on the verge of sliding into one of these ditches. Perhaps a look at these pejorative characterizations might be in order.

"Partisan" is one word we really need to examine. Isn't that what a two-party system of government is supposed to be? Our country has pretty much digested a menu of governing by two parties, with an occasional burp by a third party. The last time a third party posed any kind of a threat to the accepted two-party system was when Theodore Roosevelt mounted a surge of support for his Bull Moose Party in 1912. If the ever popular Teddy could not pull off a third party success one wonders who could. We have grown accustomed to the idea that two basic philosophies will ebb and flow over the course of time, first one prevailing and then the other, as needs and whims dictate. I think we want, or at least expect, politics to be partisan in nature, except for those times when we need to present a united front to an enemy. Otherwise we should shift to a one-party system of government.

"Negative" politics strikes us as regrettable. For most of us it is a real turn-off, especially when it occurs in the form of personal attacks or, even worse, character assassination. South Dakota is a small state and we appreciate civility, even in politics. Historically, American politics have always had a rough and tumble side. Revering Lincoln, as we do, it is shocking to discover how he was vilified in print and cartoons during his presidency. Others, with less of a halo than Lincoln, have experienced the same fate. In fact, there is less negativism in today's politics than there used to be. We have become downright polite compared to past campaigns, even the one waged between such statesmen as John Adams and Thomas Jefferson.

Honest criticism of one's opponent in politics is not only inevitable but also useful to the voter, especially when some discretion is exercised.

"Self-serving" questions the motivation of those who seek and hold office. Usually we are on thin ice when we draw conclusions about another's motives. It goes without saying that the allure of political office may have something to do with power, fame or even wealth for some. One could find plenty of examples of scoundrels who have used power for personal gain. But that could be said for every occupation. Rank politicians have no corner on dishonesty. I suppose that is why some favor "term limitations." The unfortunate side of limiting terms is that some very fine persons are excluded from doing what they do well, having grown with experience and time into their role. The best term limitation is an election. Lord Acton once said, "Power corrupts and absolute power corrupts absolutely." Every person who has power, including the politician, needs to exercise some form of self-examination to make sure he or she has not succumbed to arrogance and arbitrary disregard for the well being of others. I believe most of our politicians are honest and decent people who have a genuine desire to serve us well.

"Corrupt" is an apt description of some form of politics. American history is full of examples of big city bosses and machines, smoke filled rooms where deals are consummated, political pay-offs and voting irregularities (as in some Chicago precincts where the prevailing mood on election day was to vote early and often). All of these shady practices have given politics a black eye. However, the fact that politics can be corrupted suggests it is basically good. Only shiny, rather than rusty, metal is subject to tarnishing.

"Compromising" is a description to which politics would have to plead guilty. In fact, politics has been described as "the art of compromise." That may be alarming to those who see life only in black and white terms. It may also be disturbing to single issue purists whose sole reason for political involvement is to advance an ideological agenda to the exclusion of all other governmental agendas. They neither understand nor appreciate the "give and take" nature of political reality, sitting comfortably in the bleachers surrounded by fellow fanatics who root for the destruction of the "enemy." A strong democracy, such as ours, will survive this "loud minority" but they remain an irritation on the body politic.

So speak a good word for politics. Recognize that the political process will rub us the wrong way from time to time, that it will sometimes be abrasive, that it will foster an argument or two and that we will be absolutely amazed at the lack of good sense in the opposite camp. But stick with it. Only in a country like ours with free elections are people immersed in politics. And keep in mind the testimony of Scripture. God wants us to have a good government for our well-being. It is staggering to think that we can partner with God to help bring that about. As the various campaigns unfold, with some very attractive candidates, I might add, listen, think, maybe speak out and then vote—only once please! And be grateful for those elected politicians who see their task as a calling to serve God and their fellow Americans.

Maintenance

Those of us who grew up in small towns came close to being farm kids, but we did not quite make the grade. We spent time with our friends at their farm homes and sometimes picked up odd jobs on farms, such as shocking grain or picking potatoes, though we could always retreat to town when the going got rough.

But when I was fifteen I took a summer job with my uncle Milton who farmed four miles west of Garretson. Threshing time was the highlight of the summer. Prior to threshing we had spent several back-breaking days shocking the grain, a scratchy and sweaty task. In those days neighbors would band together and move from farm to farm to thresh each other's grain. One of the farmers owned a threshing machine, sometimes called a separator, another brought a tractor large enough to run it and all would bring their teams and hay racks. Many of the farmers took great pride in the horses they used to pull the hayracks. Some of them had matched teams. To this day I think there is nothing more beautiful than a matched pair of dapple-gray horses, though there isn't much opportunity to see that any more.

The farmers rolled into Milton's yard to begin threshing. They set the threshing machine out in the field where Milton wanted to locate his straw stack. When they had positioned the tractor at the proper distance to face the threshing machine, they hooked up the huge canvas belt to the tractor's pulley, twisted it once and wrapped it around the main pulley on the big machine. The farmers spread out in the oats field and began pitching bundles into their wagons. As the day progressed it would get to be a matter of pride as to who could load his rack the highest. When the first wagon pulled up to unload, laden with bundles, the fellow with the tractor got out his crank and started the tractor's engine. It rumbled and roared, turning the pulley and causing the threshing machine to lurch into action. It seemed to me there were hundreds of moving parts in the machine, all clanking and groaning at the same time.

The straw shot out of the blower, flying off to begin the new straw pile. The grain poured out of a smaller spout into a wagon parked next to the threshing machine. My job was to drive the old John Deere "B" and pull the wagon to the yard where the grain could be dumped on an elevator, lifted up and dropped into the granary. All in all, the whole enterprise was a team effort.

But there was more. One crew member, by no means the least important, remained in the house all day, working just as hard as the fellows out in the field. Milton's wife, Ida, was a fantastic cook and she, as did the other farm wives, outdid herself to provide mounds of food for the threshing crew. The menu included roast beef or fried chicken, heaping bowls of mashed potatoes with gravy, newly picked garden vegetables, freshly baked bread with homemade jelly and several varieties of pie—always served with egg coffee.

After dinner the men would stumble out of the house and flop down in the shade for a little nap. Then when they had watered their horses and given them a ration of oats they would go back to the field and work until the mid-afternoon lunch, which, like the mid-morning lunch, was a combination of sandwiches, pastries and coffee. Having been fed such Herculean helpings of food throughout the day, it was surprising the men made it to quitting time, at which time they dispersed to go home and do their chores. So the days passed, from one neighbor to another.

Amidst all the exciting activity and the hustle and bustle of the day there was one person who might easily go unnoticed. He may have been the most important person of the whole crew. The man who owned the threshing machine, hovering over and around it like a child with a new toy, carried a huge oil can he frequently stuck into ports on all sides of the shuddering behemoth many times each day. And if the machine malfunctioned, he would open a panel and crawl into the monster to make repairs. Without his devotion to maintenance it is not likely the threshing machine would have kept going all day, to say nothing of the whole season of threshing. His was not a striking or flashy task, but it was basic to the operation.

Maintenance of any kind is neither glamorous nor exciting but it is a necessary discipline. When the seventy-five year old high school in Oldham had to be torn down because it became structurally unsound, I asked a friend why many of our buildings seemed to have such a short life span compared to the buildings in Europe, some of which are hundreds of years old. My friend had spent a lifetime in construction, winding up as the president of a major construction company. He explained how the Europeans have developed companies who specialize in maintaining old buildings. They recognize that it is as fundamental to society to keep old buildings sound as it is to build new ones. We Americans, on the other hand, are apt to carelessly neglect basic, structural maintenance in our schools, satisfying ourselves with clean black boards and shiny floors. Meanwhile the roof weakens and the walls and foundation begin to crack and crumble.

In his letter to Titus, Paul writes, "This is a faithful saying, and these things I will that thou affirm constantly, that they which have believed in God might be careful to maintain good works." (Titus 3:8 KJV) Paul advises Titus to develop a sound plan for spiritual maintenance so that he and other Christians function as they should. What is basic to machines and buildings is also basic to God's people.

With that in mind, is it possible to summarize a Scriptural program of spiritual health maintenance? I think so, and at the risk of oversimplification I would like to present a balanced spiritual diet which would include at least four basic ingredients.

Vitamin A is ADORATION. Adoration, or worship, is basic to the Christian life. Some have described worship as "worthship," a declaration of the magnificence of God. When we praise God, in our own words or through the words of the Psalms, we are following the advice of the American philosopher, Emerson, who said "hitch your wagon to a star." We acknowledge that God alone is worthy of being praised and thereby assume a humility about the best human endeavors. We release ourselves into God's care. Worship lifts us into a world larger than ourselves and helps us see a grander picture than our eyes can pick up by scanning the world's horizon. Focusing on God, we live with a sense of mystery and awe. Life is put into proper perspective. Consider the stirring words of Psalm 95:

> "O come, let us sing to the Lord;
>   let us make a joyful noise to the rock of our salvation!

Let us come into his presence with thanksgiving;
   let us make a joyful noise to him with songs of praise!
For the Lord is a great God, and a great King above all gods.

(Ps 95:1-3)

Vitamin B is BELIEF. When Paul wrote to Timothy he included a witness to the power of trust. He writes, "…for I know whom I have believed, and am persuaded that he is able to keep that which I have committed unto him against that day." (II Timothy 1:12 KJV) Writing to the Christians in Rome, Paul mapped the pathway to salvation: "…if you confess with your lips that Jesus is Lord and believe in your heart that God raised him from the dead, you will be saved." (Romans 10:9) The word "trust" is often substituted for the word "believe" in order to capture the personal nature of faith, which is not so much a subscribing to a set of doctrinal propositions as it is a confident relationship with Jesus. One does not have to know a whole theological system to believe and trust in Jesus. The conviction that "Jesus loves me, this I know," will carry the day.

Vitamin C is CONFESSION. "Confession" is a word with two meanings. When the pastor announces the Confession of Faith in church he really means "profession." To confess one's faith is to declare the basic truths we believe. Paul uses the word in that sense when he says, "…if you confess with your lips that Jesus is Lord and believe in your heart that God raised him from the dead, you will be saved." (Romans 10:9)

The second way in which "confession" is used is more in keeping with secular usage. It means we come clean and admit we are sinful and impure and that we have sinned in thought, word and deed. Perhaps this may at first sound servile to some, but I think it is important to know that we are always in the wrong as over against God. Otherwise we may begin to believe we are justified (declared to be right) by our own goodness, at least in certain high points of our life, rather than by God's grace. By confessing our sinfulness we open the gate to God's merciful forgiveness, a canceling and energizing force. John declares, "If we confess our sins, he who is faithful and just will forgive us our sins and cleanse us from all unrighteousness." (I John 1:9)

Vitamin D is DEDICATION. Grace is free but not cheap. As the German Lutheran pastor, Dietrich Bonhoeffer, so eloquently put it, grace cost God the life of his son and it costs us obedience. Jesus called people to receive God's gifts and then to bring these same gifts of love to others. Dedication or discipleship flares off in many directions. It may mean visiting someone in trouble, giving of one's resources to a good cause, writing a devotional for one's church, smiling at a downcast stranger in the grocery line, praying for others, equipping one's self to be a witness to God's love through Bible Study, singing in the choir, running for an elective position, crusading for a clean environment and much more. Dedication takes a thousand forms. Grace is meant to flow to and through us out into the world. The fountain will never quit flowing, why should the pool not overflow? In I Corinthians 12 the apostle Paul speaks of how the Holy Spirit brings gifts to share with others to those whose faith is active and working. Then he devotes the next chapter to highlighting the greatest gift of all, love. For that reason Luther summed up the outgoing life of a Christian as "faith active in love."

Whether it be caring for a threshing machine or caring for our own spiritual lives, maintenance is often done quietly, behind the scenes. In either case it is important to keep the machine or us in working order.

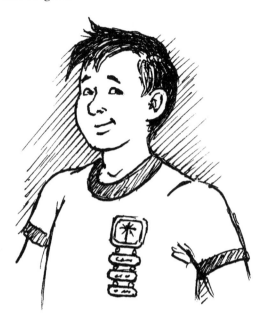

The Christmas Program

I look back on my career as a Sunday school student at Oldham Lutheran Church. It was not a distinguished career and much of it is lost in the haze of time gone by. We had no educational unit so opening exercises were held in the front of the sanctuary. Following that we dispersed to various corners of the sanctuary for classes. Many of us took pride in having perfect attendance, a feat recognized by the giving of a medal the first year and bars to hang on it for each subsequent year of steadfast loyalty. Those of us who had perfect attendance for several years looked like ostentatious Russian generals, with medals and bars hanging and clanging from our shirts or coats. The lack of up-to-date equipment or facilities was more than compensated for by the dedicated teachers. Somebody once described the best education as a teacher on one end of the log and a student on the other. Substitute "pew" for "log" and that is about what we had.

My memory is sharper when I recall the Sunday School Christmas Program. There were the inevitable, unpopular Saturday practices and spoken pieces to take home and memorize. Mother would drill me endlessly until I got both the words and the rhythm right. She would have agreed with Aristotle who said, "It is not sufficient to know what one ought to say, but one must also know how to say it." When it came to saying the piece at the program I could never hold a candle to my friend Nels. He had powerful vocal chords and just the right Norwegian modulation to fill the church with his rhythmical voice. We had no microphones, but everyone heard Nels. After hearing Nels speak his piece, there were many who predicted he would go into the ministry.

One year I had to fight off an unholy pride when I was chosen to play Joseph in the traditional pageant, complete, as always, with a manger scene. I wore a bathrobe of course, but where it came from I don't know. We boys in our house had no such luxury. I do not recall who played Mary, but I am sure we had a bond that lasted for some time. For kids the line between acting and reality is fuzzy. In recent years some churches have gone to scripted programs with scant reference to a manger scene. Then I am never sure whether I have been to a Christmas program or not.

Then, as now, the church was packed for the event. In those days the church and the school were the social centers of the community. Not only did parents and grandparents show up for the Christmas program, but practically everyone else did too. Flash cameras and video cameras were not yet on the scene so the audience had fewer distractions with which to contend. Most parents sat in silent terror, fearing it would be their child who might forget the words to the piece. Following the program the church presented all of the children with a large sack of candy. There was no dentist in Oldham to throw cold water on the practice. The huge pieces of hard candy, curling back and forth, were a wonderful treat. The praise we received from our parents and the candy were more than adequate compensation for those grueling Saturday practices and the nervous tension we experienced in front of so many people.

I would like to think those Christmas programs were more than cute or entertaining. I hope they accomplished more than providing a boost to parental pride.

For one thing they were a part of a long tradition, one which continues to this day. Traditions give stability and identity to a community or family. A tradition is a possession, prized by those who have it as much as a precious jewel. It may be complicated or simple, no matter. It is there and one can count on it. It does not have to be explained or justified, just celebrated. People, young and old, men and women, are brought together through traditions as generation after generation repeats the event, remembering the past and anticipating the future. To defend a tradition by saying "this is what we have always done" is not stupid or regressive. It may be that a statement like that represents one of the more progressive ideas we have ever expressed.

A tradition is even more profound when it is full of meaningful content. A Christmas program tells a story, an old story with an always new twist. And there is no one we would rather hear the story from than our children. It is a simple story and we know they are getting it as well as telling it. They remind us of the gift of a lifetime. "For God so loved the world that he gave his only son," they tell us in word and song and (these days) lots of action. It gives us hope for the future of both the church and the world. These are the children who will some day be teaching Sunday School, serving on church boards, sewing quilts for the mission field, singing or ringing in our choirs, filling our pulpits and going to Sunday School Christmas Programs to watch and hear their children tell the old, old story of Jesus and his love.

Looking Back

It was turning out to be a sad day even before I looked back.

We all have our sacred places. One of mine is a cemetery four miles west of Garretson, called Norway Cemetery. There my great-grandparents, my grandparents, my brother, my nephew and other relatives rest. Periodically I pay a visit to Norway to spend some time with forbears I never knew and others I knew very well. I have gone there more often since my younger brother passed away three years ago. I wander from grave to grave, touching the monuments, bringing flowers, reminiscing, pondering and brooding. My grandparents chose this as their final resting place because it was adjacent to their church, Norway Lutheran Church. A number of years ago the congregation disbanded and not long after that the church building burned to the ground. Later, my brother, Paul, chose Norway cemetery for his burial place because it is a beautiful setting, with a commanding view in all directions of the rolling hills of Minnehaha County. It is a perfect place to greet the sunrise and admire the sunset.

I had spent the better part of an hour there, alone with my thoughts and my memories. While the summer breeze murmured in the tall evergreens, I recalled moments with Paul, my grandparents, Uncle Milton, and others. Leaving, I drove east to the Corson road, then south to the Midway road, then west to old highway 77. This would not be helpful to a stranger. You have to already know where you are and where you are going to fathom these directions. Having driven less than a mile on the Midway road, I turned and looked back over my shoulder to the place where my grandparents had lived. Every building except the chicken coop is gone now. New buildings occupy the space, except for the large grove, which remains intact.

It dawned on me, as I looked back, that of the six people whom I identify with that farm, I am the only one left. My grandparents died in the 1960s, my folks in the '70s and my brother, Paul, three years ago. The farm had been our family destination every Christmas, Thanksgiving and summer. I began spending summers there at the age of six and Paul, four years younger than I, joined me when he hit six. Mother was an only child and that meant there weren't any cousins with which to share the place—or, now, its memories.

In time I suppose I could describe all the things we did and how we did them. But words would not be sufficient to capture all of the nuances of that place and those years. I would eventually give up trying to convey the sounds, smells and sights of the farm. I could name a few colors, but not the shades. I could describe the cloth, but not the many textures. It dawned on me that being the sole survivor means more than having outlived the others. It also means that there will be locked up within me images and experiences which I cannot fully share with anyone else. I lack the ability to bring that part of the past fully alive and others are not that much interested either. If I think too much about it I detect a developing loneliness coming over me. I make the decision not to forget but also not to persist in looking back. I begin to focus on the future as I drive west.

Thoughts about the future include my children and grandchildren, my church and my community, others I care about and me. There are some worries that accompany a focus on the future and it lacks a complete, concrete picture but it does pull one out of melancholy isolation. And it does move one to prayer and action.

I have recalled that moment of looking back many times. It has caused me to recognize that we are fortunate to be able to remember the past in the company of those who share that past. Each of us has a bank of memories. When others possess the same memories there can be a sharing beyond the words we use to recall them. Others are right there with us. They can fill in all the gaps and provide the setting from their memory banks. That would likely be true at a reunion of one's college class, for example.

But suppose we attended a reunion of a class that had graduated ten years later. We would feel completely out of place, not because we were ten years older but rather because there would be no common memories. In vain we would search for someone with whom we could knowingly trade stories. Our memories would remain locked within us as we made small talk with strangers.

I have wondered if that is not the way the gospel writers felt when they realized their experiences with Jesus were shared by fewer and fewer as their contemporaries passed on. John may have spoken for all of them when he wrote, "Now Jesus did many other signs in the presence of his disciples, which are not written in this book. But these are written so that you may come to believe that Jesus is the Messiah, the Son of God, and that through believing you may have life in his name." (John 20:30,31)

How to convey the memories was the question. Details would be important. Impressions would count. Conversations would matter. Actions as well as words ought to be included. Reactions of others would be crucial. The writers of the gospels carefully incorporated all of these elements and more in telling the story of Jesus. It was as though they were building a memory of Jesus for succeeding generations to make their own.

The song writer asked the musical question, "Were You There When They Crucified My Lord?" The gospel writers reflect the same concern, though it is not in the form of a question. They wanted us to be there as Jesus called disciples, told those wonderful parables, healed the sick and befriended the friendless. They wanted us to be there in the house with Mary and Martha, at the Wedding in Cana and with the sleeping disciples in the Garden of Gethsamane. They thought we should know about how Jesus lost his cool in the temple, how he patiently helped Thomas to believe and how he died.

Those who talk to others about Jesus always find it easier to do so when they are speaking to persons with a Biblical memory. Then, communication is more like a sharing than a monologue. The bearer of the story and the hearer of the story have both been there. They remember. They can make the connections.

Is there a better argument for telling the Bible stories to our children? Each story becomes a deposit we make on their behalf in their memory bank. Some day they can make a withdrawal. Faith requires knowledge of Jesus. We cannot force faith into our children but we can equip them with the stories. Even when faith is delayed it eventually builds upon those stories. The stories are the roots and faith is the flower.

The church is made up of those who have a common memory which they regularly share with one another. All of us have 'been there" with Jesus because of the way in which the gospel writers have so richly described him and the setting for his mission and message. To go it without the church, even though one is a believer, is to feel the isolation and even loneliness of one who is, so to speak, the last one standing.

The Falls

There was a time when the Falls of the Sioux River and nearby Seney Island drew the citizens of Sioux Falls like a magnet. Each provided a lovely setting for picnics and a host of other social gatherings. People came for rest, relaxation and renewal to these two sanctuaries.

But "Progress" was in the air in the early days of Sioux Falls, and it was marked by commercial growth. First the railroad came and in the name of progress cut off Seney Island from the rest of the city. Then, in order to provide power to a new, spacious mill (the Queen Bee Mill), the city authorized the building of a dam which flooded part of Seney Island. In 1907 the city built a hydroelectric plant, raising the dam by two feet and extending it to cut off the channel that surrounded Seney Island. Between 1907 and 1924 the city encouraged developers to fill in the channel around what was left of the once beautiful and busy Island. The railroad then offered to buy the Island in order to build a turn table, coal bins and a water tower. By then the river moved nearly as much sewage as water. Smoke, steam and obnoxious odors drifted across the Sioux River, Seney Island and the Falls of the Sioux. Progress had arrived, reckless and careless in all of its works and all its ways.

Around 1924, a handful of old timers who were interested in redefining progress as something that did not have to destroy natural beauty in order to succeed formed a County Historical Society. They suggested to the mayor that the city ought to buy the island, remembering the time when it had served as a sanctuary for the busy and hard working citizens of Sioux Falls. The mayor disagreed, saying it would more than likely become a hangout for bums.

Enter Richard Pettigrew, once known as the "Pickerel Senator," probably because of his aggressive approach to issues he believed to be important. Pettigrew wrote a now famous letter to the mayor stating his belief that the former Seney Island and its environs should be converted into a public park. He also advocated extending a road from downtown to the Falls and using the land east of the road to create that park. He did not mention anything about building some sort of gate or archway to mark the road but, observing the beautiful gate of petrified wood he built at the entrance to Woodlawn Cemetery, it is not difficult to imagine such a thought may have been in the back of his mind.

Pettigrew wrote that letter in 1924. For the better part of eighty years it was ignored. But now, in 2004, Pettigrew's dream has come true. Sometimes it takes a while for an idea to germinate. The City of Sioux Falls has redis-covered its natural soul. The Falls of the Sioux are once again the heart of the city. While Seney Island has not been recreated, the "Phillips to the Falls" project has achieved a union of the City with the Falls. It also pro-vides another beautiful space along the River where people may once again gather for rest, relaxation and renewal. An archway will greet the traveler from one destination to the other, signaling one's approach to either down-town or the Falls of the Sioux—not so much to provide direction as to celebrate the journey.

I thought of this sequence of events while studying the Biblical text about John the Baptist, found in Matthew 3:1-12.

The Baptist's scathing condemnation of the religious condition suggests a river of grace polluted by human pride. He addressed the religious leaders by calling them a "brood of vipers," a pack of snakes. By presenting them-selves to be baptized, they made a mockery of authentic religion which, in the best tradition of the prophets, should have been displayed through humility and a seeking after justice for all. Their focus was on lineage rather than service. They took great pride in claiming Abraham as their father but found it difficult to see themselves as God's needy and dutiful children. Nobody was looking up. They looked back and were proud to claim Abraham for themselves and they looked around, armed with their moral measurements, to see who was the fairest of them all. In the process they damned the river of grace and covered up the spaces where people could be renewed and find peace. God's shaded island of love and peace had become inaccessible.

Enter John the Baptist, looking and speaking the part of the best of the Old Testament prophets. Like those old prophets, he was out of season. They were famous for voicing a negative message when things seemed to be going smoothly and a soft and tender word when life was rough. Whoever described a newspaper's role as afflicting the comfortable and comforting the afflicted pretty much described the prophets too.

John dreamed of building a road which would help to reclaim the souls of those who dwelt in the city of God. His road would not be circuitous or complicated. It would lead straight to the Falls of God's flowing mercy, where grace upon grace cascaded and washed over the rocks of human sin and formed a pool of forgiveness. He called for the building of a "Gate of Repentance," through which those who sought God's blessings could pass with contrite hearts. He assured the people they would know it when they saw this beautiful scene, a wonderful manifestation of God's presence among them.

John wanted the people to see Jesus, who was now ready to begin his task, one which would take him all the way to his cross. In the presence of Jesus, people could relax. They would not have to tally their merits or wring their hands over their demerits. They would not have to wonder if they had done enough good or too much bad. Each person need only travel the new road to the "Rock of Ages" with the same frame of mind later captured by the hymn writer, "Nothing in my hand I bring, simply to thy cross I cling."

A summary of the parallel tracks we have been on, while admittedly a bit forced, might be helpful.

There was a mess. The Sioux River, the Falls and its environs were allowed to deteriorate into a bedraggled state which was difficult to find and unrewarding to those who made the effort.

There was a man. Richard Pettigrew declared his vision of a road, straight and true, that would go from the heart of the city to the Falls and a plan for beautifying the surroundings.

There was a goal. The desire of those who had the vision was to once again bring the people of Sioux Falls to a place of great natural beauty and thereby help them to find inspiration and a sense of who they were.

There was a mess. Religion had succumbed to a proud recitation of heritage and a recapitulation of human achievement. It was hard to know where God fit into that kind of agenda. Souls were empty.

There was a man. John the Baptist declared his vision of a road, straight and true, that would bring people back to a strong relationship with God. He insisted there would have to be a gate, called "Repentance," through which the travelers must pass in order to proceed.

There was a goal. John was a pointer. He wanted people to quickly look past him and see the one to whom he was pointing. Travel the road, he encouraged, and behold the "Rock of Ages." Having found Jesus, experience the rest and renewal to be found in him, John declared. Those who found the Rock would be so overwhelmed they would insist it was more accurate to say the Rock had found them.

The road is there. Try it.

Pioneers

Were it not for a breach of trust I might not be here. In fact, I might not be anywhere. My second cousin, Ray Loftesness, uncovered a sordid tale of intrigue when he traveled to Norway and started asking questions about our family. It seems my great-great grandfather could neither read nor write. So, when it came time for him to make a will, he asked the local clergyman to assist him in listing the heirs to whom he would give his land. After my great-great grandfather passed away and the will was read his family was shocked to discover the farm had been willed to the clergyman's daughter instead of the rightful heirs. The pastor had swindled them out of a farm.

Whether my great grandparents, Johannes and Britha Loftesness, would have eventually come to this country had there been no trickery is open to speculation. As it turned out, they really had no choice for there was nothing left for them to do in Norway. Johannes was a farmer without any land or resources to buy land. Compared to their lot in Norway, America truly was the land of opportunity.

But the opportunity was not handed to them on a silver platter. They came to southeastern Minnesota where they stayed long enough to catch their breath. Then they headed west in an eleven covered wagon caravan. In 1873 they arrived in Dakota Territory and staked out a claim for one hundred and sixty acres of land in eastern Minnehaha County, west of Garretson. Two shallow recessions can still be seen on this property, marking the spot near a ravine where Johannes and Britha built a sod house and barn. The document he signed to claim the land is still on file in the courthouse. His signature is beautifully written and by it there is an "X," suggesting the possibility that a clerk signed his name for him. Probably Johannes, like his father, could neither read nor write. He was fifty-five years old when he came to Dakota Territory.

In his novel, *Giants In The Earth*, Ole Rolvaag described the struggle of those early pioneers who came to Dakota Territory in 1873. Rolvaag relied on first hand information from his father-in-law, Andrew Berdahl, who had come in the same covered wagon caravan as my great grandparents. Aside from the fact that the novel is a classic, I find it compelling because of the attachment to my ancestors.

Rolvaag painted a picture of the immigrants, particularly the main characters, Per Hansa and his wife, Beret, struggling and surviving. The pioneers felt overwhelmed by the vastness of the formless prairie. Beret wondered how human beings could endure this place, where there was nothing to hide behind. Compared to the mountains and the sea of Norway the prairie had "no heart that beat, no waves that sang, no soul that could be touched . . . or cared." On the other hand, they had never in all their lives seen such great sunsets.

Nor had they ever seen such vicious blizzards. In the end, it was a blizzard that finally conquered the indomitable Per Hansa. In the midst of a howling blizzard he set out on skis to find a pastor to minister to his ailing neighbor. He never returned. In the spring a troop of young boys looking for stray cattle found the frozen body of Per Hansa leaning up against a haystack with his skis beside him. His sunken eyes were set toward the west, a symbol of hope in the future. Even in death this optimistic and energetic man conveyed a life force.

Beret, on the other hand, found the prairie to be increasingly forbidding as she struggled with demons both real and imaginary. She gradually sank into depression, a condition not uncommon to pioneer women who had left homeland and family behind without the same commitment as their husbands. As Per Hansa revealed Beret's condition to the pastor, he explained that Beret had never felt at home in America. There are some people, he thought, who should never emigrate because "they can't take pleasure in that which is to come—they simply can't see it." Beret began to emerge from her depression after the pastor celebrated the sacrament of Holy Communion for the settlement in her home and also after she overheard Per Hansa express confidence in her ability to care for her children—affirmation from both God and man.

Rolvaag continued the story of Beret and their son, Peder, in two later novels, *Peder Victorious* and *Their Fathers' God*. In fact Beret emerges as one of the strongest characters in all of American fiction. These novels reflect that as the years went by the pioneers' struggle was less against the natural forces and more against social and religious issues that threatened to undo them. Rolvaag had hoped that Norwegian immigrants would not be swallowed up by their new country to the extent they would lose their identity as Norwegians. He had no enthusiasm for the so-called "melting pot" theory, where every immigrant group lost its uniqueness. He rather favored the concept of what might be called a "simmering stew," all in one pot but with the ingredients recognizable and distinguishable. And maybe even "tasteable!"

Fortunately, at least one of the members of that 1873 covered wagon caravan from southeastern Minnesota wrote an autobiography. Erick Berdahl's story, written in 1925, has been privately published by his family and copyrighted by Richard Brown. It's a fascinating account of pioneer life and a treasure for the Berdahl family. One's heart aches for Erick and his wife Hannah as he details the birth and, too often, the death of each child. He describes the birth of their nine children and how five of them died between the ages of two and six from various diseases. Maybe the saddest entry is the one describing the death of their oldest daughter, Christine, who died of complications from pregnancy at the age of twenty-four. Only three of their nine children lived to the time Erick wrote his story. One looks for clues to discover how this couple survived all of these tragedies. Clearly there is a sense of resignation. Life was fragile in those days. Mortality was in the very air they breathed. But it was their faith in God's care that provided the needed solace. After their third child, Anna, passed away they found comfort in their Christian Faith: "In the midst of our grief we knew that our dear ones that were taken away by death at that age were safely in the heavens above with their Lord and Savior."

Tom Brokaw wrote a book about the Second World War generation which he titled *The Greatest Generation*. Some in that generation have disputed the description, citing the notion that all generations carry seeds of greatness that flower when the appropriate challenge presents itself. Ole Rolvaag paid a like tribute to the pioneer generation he described in his novels. In the last chapter of *Giants In The Earth* he wrote, "The human race has not known such faith and such self-confidence since history began." Clearly, facing the loneliness of leaving home, the strangeness of a new country and the hardships of the northern prairie required a huge amount of courage and character. One could hardly overstate the case for calling the pioneers "great."

I think, however, the pioneers' values were such that they would not quibble over which was the greatest of all the generations. They would be more inclined to suggest we emulate those qualities we find compelling in every generation and face with courage whatever challenges we find in our path. As the author of the New Testament Letter to the Hebrews suggests, these heroes of courage and faith, who now rest from their labors, make up a vast cheering section in the heavenly bleachers. (Hebrews 12:1) We are still running the race, but has anyone had better fans than these?

The Light House

You didn't know Oldham had a light house did you?

No, this was not one of those light houses you picture standing by the sea on the rocky coast of Maine. This was not a light house steeped in lore and credited for saving storm tossed sailors at sea. This was more like a lighted house. But if you had been lost out there on the prairie west of Oldham you would have had a beacon to guide you into a safe haven.

My parents did not leave my brother and me alone in the dark very often. I vividly recall the first time it happened and mother's retelling of the story kept that memory alive. I suppose I was nine or ten. My brother was 4 years younger than I. That meant that I was in charge, though I felt more vulnerable than a protector should. The big two-story house on the west edge of town that served as the Lutheran parsonage was our home. It had 48 windows. As the hours of darkness passed during that night of ultimate responsibility, I became increasingly afraid. To dispel my fear I went about the house and turned on every light switch I could find on all three levels of the house. The house was lit up like a tilted pinball machine. People approaching town from the west must have wondered what kind of public event was taking place. As they got close enough to identify the house they may have wondered if the Lutheran pastor was maybe hosting a wild party or an orgy, even. That would have been a gift from heaven to those who liked to talk.

When my parents returned they had no idea of what to make of the spectacle they observed as they drove into the driveway. Naturally they were glad to find us alive and well, if a bit scared. As my father went from room to room and flicked off the lights my mother sat with me in the kitchen to settle me down. Knowing her thoughtful ways, I'm sure she both complimented and corrected me. After all, I had kept both of us safe! A soaring electrical bill meant little to me.

What is there about light that gives us courage? When John in his gospel describes the coming of Jesus he uses the metaphor of light. Jesus, John proclaims, was the light of all people. And this "light shines in the darkness, and the darkness did not overcome it." (John 1:5)

Later, in the same gospel, John quotes Jesus who describes himself as the "light of the world." "Whoever follows me," says Jesus, "will never walk in darkness but will have the light of life." (John 8:12) The kind of sight to which Jesus referred may be thought of as insight, a way of seeing what life is all about.

In his first letter, possibly written slightly after his Gospel, John gives one of the few definitions of God found in the Bible. "...God is light and in him is no darkness at all," says John. (I John 1:5) To live our life in that light is to "have fellowship with one another" and to know that "the blood of Jesus his Son cleanses us from all sin." (I John 1:7) The implication is that we have a choice in the matter. We can choose darkness if we wish by sidestepping Jesus, the light of the world.

Heaven knows that parsonage on the west side of Oldham had known the shadows of darkness. I often had less than perfect fellowship with the Lord, my parents or my brother. My father had his own ways to remind me I was out of fellowship, usually by applying his palm to my butt in quick and forceful motions. It was called spanking. There were times I welcomed whatever darkness I could manage as a cover for my snitching. My father stored the communion wine in a dark room in the basement and more than once I slipped in to sample the forbidden beverage. So far as I know my parents never discovered that indiscretion. I was not so lucky when it came to the little store room upstairs. There mother kept a variety of food items, including a jar or two of maraschino cherries and the always delicious chocolate chips. Apparently mother had a better handle on her inventory of delicacies than my father did on his communion wine because she always seemed to know when I had sampled her goodies. She understood boys though, and I never got more than a mild lecture from her. I suppose that is why I went for the cherries and chips more often than the wine. Besides, they tasted better.

What is there about light that caused Jesus to use it as a way to describe himself? And why did John pick up the metaphor and run with it? The Genesis creation story begins with God creating light. Light is a necessary condition for life to exist. John's gospel is an account of God's second creation where, in Jesus, God gives everyone a new beginning. The apostle Paul pushes this theme beyond the usual meanings of a new beginning by describing those in Christ as new creations. But the light must come first in order to overcome all the inner and outer darkness of the world. The chaos of unbelief and self-will must first be vanquished if life is to flourish. So God brings light into our dark world—the "light of the world."

Then too, there could be no growth without light. We know how it works in the natural world. Plants must have light if they are going to grow. No rose has ever blossomed in a cave. The amount of light, or length of the day, is what triggers the blossoming of plants and the mating of birds. Light is not only a background for life, it is a life force. Of course, as a master teacher Jesus provides light on a variety of themes. But it is primarily his presence and his touch that brings growth-causing light into our lives.

Light radiates warmth, reducing the chills of life. More than once I have hunkered down behind a pine tree in the pre-dawn darkness of a spring morning in the Black Hills while I called turkeys. I was primed to welcome a strutting gobbler making his way toward me. But after an hour or so of shivering in the cold I was even more anxious to greet the sun and let its beams bring warmth back into my body. As the sun rose in the east it first hit the tree tops. Then, all too slowly, the light slipped down the tree to the ground and finally touched me with its warming rays. Similarly, Jesus brings a warming comfort to us amidst the chills of life, even thawing the iciness of our own hearts from time to time.

Light also makes sight possible. One of the first Bible passages I memorized as a child was Psalm 119:105: "Your word is a lamp to my feet and a light to my path." How would we get along in life without light? At night, when the sun does not provide our light, we find a way to artificially lighten our way through electricity and, sometimes, fire. Without light we could never read or see each other or find our way anywhere. But there is a higher kind of light, of a spiritual nature, which we also desperately need. Even on a sparkling, bright day or amidst the dazzling lights of our creation at night we may be walking in spiritual darkness. Enveloped by a darkness that knows no God and no purpose to life, we stumble from one day to another. When Jesus told us that he had come in order that we might have life he could just as well have said he had come so that we might have light. After all he is the "light of the world" and the light of our lives. In him we see God, ourselves and each other well enough to get a good handle on life and know where we are going, or should be going, and how to get there. He lights up our life.

Long ago in that big house on the west side of Oldham I found great comfort in the lights that pushed out every dark and fearful shadow. Today, as an adult, I find great comfort in being surrounded by the One who is Light, experiencing how the shadows of life are forced back away from me.

Gossip

As cows are to Texas, so is gossip to a small town. Many a sentence has begun with the words "Did you hear…" To be the subject, if not the victim, of gossip is one of the prices a person pays for living in a small town. Depending on how malicious the gossip is, one may pay a very high price. It is perhaps the chosen weapon among the lowly for bringing down the high and mighty. Possibly it is also the favored technique of the high and mighty for keeping the lowly in their place. Such gossip can range from fanciful stories with no factual basis whatsoever to stories with a germ of truth but embellished with the kind of creative fiction worthy of a Pulitzer Prize. Mischievous and false gossip has made life miserable for many in small communities. More than a few loose tongued folks have managed to achieve self esteem by spreading bad tidings about others.

I have a friend who, years ago as a college student, telephoned home to talk to her mother about her wedding plans. Her folks were on a party line, which meant others overheard the entire conversation. She happened to mention that she favored a wedding dress of her favorite color, frosty blue. Not long after that telephone chat with her mother she received a call from her grandmother who had picked up the word on the street that her granddaughter was pregnant. Someone had falsely drawn the conclusion that her desire for a non-white wedding dress provided an air tight implication of pregnancy and reported it as fact.

Perhaps that was the kind of gossip about which Paul warned Timothy. Paul thought young widows were the most likely ones to engage in idle gossip and therefore suggested they be encouraged to marry and busy themselves with parental and household duties so they would not go "gadding about from house to house." (I Timothy 5:13) The author of Proverbs also discouraged the practice of gossiping and, at the same time, commended those who could keep a confidence:

> "Whoever belittles another
>   lacks sense,
> but an intelligent person
>   remains silent.
>
> A gossip goes about telling
>   secrets,
> but one who is trustworthy
>   in spirit keeps a
>   confidence." (Proverbs 11:12,13)

The eighth commandment warns against bearing false witness against one's neighbor. When Luther included the commandments in his *Small Catechism* he provided an explanation to each one. He explained the eighth commandment in the following way:

> "We should fear and love God that we may not deceitfully belie, betray, slander or defame our neighbor, but defend him, speak well of him, and put the best construction on everything."

The second part of Luther's explanation suggests the possibility of good gossip. He did not rule out the practice of talking about others, but suggested whatever words one speaks about others ought to improve their standing, rather than tarnish it.

So what about the good gossip? In her wonderful book, *Dakota*, Kathleen Norris wrote what she described as a "spiritual geography." She had returned from the East Coast to live in her ancestral home of Lemmon, South Dakota, where she encountered the dynamics of small town life, including the prevalence of gossip. Norris named a chapter "The Holy Use of Gossip," in which she argued that the right kind of gossip can strengthen communal bonds. She acknowledged that some gossip is vicious and cruel. But good gossip, she suggested, is the glue that holds a community together. Norris's thoughts about the positive role of gossip struck a chord with me. I recalled the many conversations among adults about other people I overheard as a kid. I thought of my grandmother telling my grandfather all the tidbits of information about neighbors she had picked up by listening on the telephone party line. Other wives and husbands were doing the same thing and by so doing applying some sort of cement which bonded them all together, for better or for worse.

I recalled my mother and her friends talking about others in my little hometown of Oldham, sometimes critically, often in praise, but usually quite objectively. It seemed to me to be a form of neighborliness encouraged by the local paper, *The Oldham Register*, where all sorts of personal news notes appeared in print. The practice continues to this day. Even though many small towns have lost their local paper there are those whose task it is to ferret out the news and report it to a larger paper which includes news from surrounding towns. When somebody visits a neighbor on a Sunday evening it is reported. People who are grateful for favors name and thank their benefactors through the paper. Birthdays are noted, as are the folks who attended the birthday party. A good deal of poetic license is allowed. I once shot a nice (but not spectacular) buck up north of Oldham. By the time Lyla, the local reporter, got it into the paper it became "one of the largest bucks ever shot in Kingsbury County." She never saw the buck, but relied on an overly enthusiastic third party account. She was also "in my corner," so to speak, since she thought of me as her fourth son. A small town is not a place to live if you are seeking privacy or even, sometimes, objectivity.

But a small town is a great place to live if one wants to "practice" the art of Christian neighborliness. Where better than where people live in such close and familiar proximity to one another? In the city we may hardly know the names of our neighbors and rarely even greet them, unless we are mowing our lawns at the same time. But in a small town rich and poor, young and old and women and men constantly rub shoulders with one another. James Baldwin once wrote a book called *Nobody Knows My Name*. In the small town in which I grew up everybody knew my name. The grapevine was so effective that my folks would have done no better had they paid someone to shadow me.

I recently conducted a Bible Study at First Lutheran Church in which we explored how Christian love works by looking at thirty-three of the "One Anothers" of Scripture. I will list them without comment, except to point out how adaptable they are to living in a small community, whether that community be a small town or a Christian congregation.

1. Love one another (John 13:34)
2. Members of one another (Romans 12;5)
3. Outdo one another [in showing honor] (Romans 12:10)
4. Wash one another's feet [a sign of hospitality] (John 13:14)
5. Rejoice with one another (Romans 12:15, I Corinthians 12:26)
6. Weep with one another (Romans 12:15)
7. Live in harmony with one another (Romans 12:16)
8. Don't judge one another (Romans 14:13)
9. Welcome one another (Romans 15:7)
10. Admonish one another (Colossians 3:16)
11. Greet one another (Romans 16;16)
12. Wait for one another (I Corinthians 11:33)
13. Care for one another (I Corinthians 12:25)
14. Serve one another (Galatians 5:13; I Peter 4:10)
15. Be kind to one another (Ephesians 4:32)
16. Forgive one another (Ephesians 4:32; Colossians 3:13)
17. Be compassionate toward one another (Ephesians 4:32)
18. Encourage one another (I Thessalonians 5:11)
19. Submit to one another (Ephesians 5:21)
20. Bear with one another (Ephesians 4:2; Colossians 3:13)
21. Stimulate love in one another (Hebrews 10:24)
22. Offer hospitality to one another (I Peter 4:9)
23. Be clothed in humility towards one another (I Peter 5:5)
24. Don't slander one another (James 4:11)
25. Don't grumble against one another (James 5:9)
26. Confess your sins to one another (James 5:16)
27. Pray for one another (James 5:16)
28. Fellowship with one another (I John 1:7)
29. Don't be puffed up against one another (I Corinthians 4:6)
30. Carry one another's burdens (Galatians 6:2)
31. Honor one another (Romans 12:10)
32. Instruct one another (Romans 15:14)
33. Comfort one another (II Corinthians 1:4)

Scripture makes it clear that, while religion is always personal, it is not meant to be private. Our faith should reach out to others and somehow reflect God's love for them. The "One Another" admonitions assume an interaction between people—perhaps one best achieved in a community where people not only watch and talk about one another but also watch out for one another and talk about one another in the graceful tones of gratitude for the gift of neighbors, imperfect though they may be. "Holy gossip" may, in fact, be the necessary and informative prelude to stepping forth and offering a hand. It would not be too far-fetched to suggest that every community can be thought of as a mission field where we not only share news about one another but also can embody the Good News for one another.

Determination

He called and suggested we meet in the lobby of our hospital in Watertown. I found his east coast accent and rapid delivery to be intriguing. He was, to use "prairie speak," a good talker.

After all these years I have forgotten his name. I don't recall how he acquired my name or office number but he was there in the lobby waiting for me. He was unshaven but otherwise clean and he wore jeans and a shirt that was once attractive but was now a bit worse for the wear. He had a good story. He had come from the East Coast, he said, and tomorrow someone would be coming through Watertown to pick him up. Then he would go on to Montana where he had a job waiting. He explained that he was an accountant transitioning to a new job. In the meantime he needed some financial help, which he had figured down to the last penny (wouldn't you expect that from an accountant?)—enough to get a hotel room, a meal at a grocery store and a pack of cigarettes. It would be a matter of a few weeks and he would repay the loan, he promised. He just had to get his feet on the ground again.

I began my usual spiel in dealing with such a request. I told him we had agencies in town, which all the churches supported, to help stranded travelers. I had come to appreciate the "street smarts" of the folks who regularly handled such requests for help. Besides, it was a good way to put a stop to the practice of many supplicants who went from church to church, changing their religion in a matter of a few blocks. He didn't want to bother with all of that fussing, he argued. I countered with a partial truth. I said I didn't have enough money at the moment to extend personal charity. He reminded me that he wasn't asking for the moon, suggesting I was a bit stingy for even hesitating. Then I gave him my best argument for withholding financial help. I pointed out that of all the people who had received help from me or my church and had promised to pay back their loan, none had. He looked me in the eye and answered me with a line I will never forget. "So you don't get paid back," he said, "what will you do, lower the flags to half-mast and call for a national day of mourning?"

I gave him the money. His determination was impressive. His performance was so good it deserved some kind of reward. I had paid more money and been less entertained. That was about twenty-five years ago. I am still waiting to hear from him, but not holding my breath. I hope he's doing well and likes Montana. Probably if every one who had succumbed to his persistent and unorthodox method of raising personal funds got together we would be a sizeable community with some good stories. We would all have had one lesson in artful determination even though it may not have been the most desirable usage of such a trait.

Not long ago I received a letter from Vera, the mother of one of my boyhood friends, now living in DeSmet. She is well advanced in years now but still independent enough to drive her own car. She wanted to make sure I would be at her funeral in one capacity or another. Aside from that request she shared other tidbits of news. Her letter came shortly after Easter and so the events of that day were fresh in her mind. She had been driving herself to church for the Easter service when she encountered a train. This is how she described it: "As I was waiting for a train my car stopped and as I tried to start it [it] caught fire and burned up. Some friends came and took me to church." I have this mental picture now of this determined woman standing beside her flaming car by the railroad tracks with only one concern—how will she get to church? No doubt, it has been that kind of undeterred determination which has contributed to her long life.

Of the two stories of determination I have just related I suppose the second one is the more commendable. Persistence in getting to church to worship and to give thanks for the Resurrection of Jesus is a testimony to all of us. Yet, I find the first one to ring with Biblical overtones as well. For, after all, we are all beggars in the presence of God.

Jesus told two stories I have never completely understood. In one of the stories a man received guests whom he was unprepared to host. So he goes to his friend at midnight, wakes him up and asks him to lend three loaves. But his sleepy friend cannot conceal his disgust with being awakened. He protests that to get up now would likely wake his children and besides he has already locked the door. It sounds like this was a very shallow friendship. Eventually he does as requested, not because of the friendship between the two but because the supplicant has been persistent. (Luke 11:5-9)

In the second and somewhat similar story Jesus told of a crusty judge who did not care much either for God or for people. A widow repeatedly came to him asking for justice against her adversary. For a while the judge refused but eventually he caved in, not, said Jesus, because he cared a lick for either God or the widow but because he was tired of being bothered by her. He granted her request in order to get the determined woman out of his hair. (Luke 18:1-5)

Jesus told both stories to highlight the importance of determination in our prayers. The so-called friend who had been asleep before he was awakened at midnight and the unjust judge represent God. The friend with the unexpected guests and the injured widow represent us. I wish God had not been represented by those two unattractive characters because Scripture is clear that God is ready to forgive us at the drop of a prayer. Nevertheless it does remind us that in interpreting the parables of Jesus we should look for one main point and not press too hard on the other details.

And the point of both stories is to be persistent in our praying and never to lose heart. As an explanation of the first of these two parables Jesus said:

> "So I say to you, Ask, and it will be given you; search, and you will find; knock, and the door will be opened for you. For everyone who asks receives, and everyone who searches finds, and for everyone who knocks, the door will be opened." (Luke 11:9,10)

These words of Jesus present a picture of someone coming to a strange town in order to look up an old friend. He may first stop at a gas station in order to ask directions to a certain street and otherwise get the lay of the land. Then, directions in hand, he will seek out that address, maybe taking a wrong turn or two in the process but eventually he finds his friend's house. He parks his car, walks up to the front door and knocks. The door is opened and two old friends stand face to face. His determination has been rewarded.

Some have attempted to practice a persistent prayer life by reciting throughout the day what has been called the "Jesus Prayer." The prayer is both simple and profound: "Lord Jesus, have mercy on me." It isn't that God has a short attention span and must constantly be reminded that we have our needs but that we are people who often are distracted to the point that we forget our needs. When Jesus asks us to be determined seekers, or should I say beggars, he does so for our sakes, not God's. God is always focused, we are not. To clarify what great mercy we want from God is more for our benefit than God's. And God won't mind if, by our determination, we sometimes become a bit brazen.

Music

Charles Dickens opened his novel, *A Tale of Two Cities*, with the enigmatic sentence, "It was the best of times, it was the worst of times, it was the age of wisdom, it was the age of foolishness . . ." My thoughts about music may, to some degree, reflect what Dickens had to say about the times he described in his novel. Looking at it one way, I am totally unqualified to discuss the subject of music, having no real skills or training in music. But, seeing it from another direction, I am at least moderately qualified, particularly when it comes to thoughts about the role of music in the church. I love music and as a non-musician I probably represent the vast majority in any congregation. So the reader may continue, knowing there may very well be a mixture in what follows of stupidity and wisdom, ignorance and knowledge, naivety and savvy.

My music resume is unimpressive. In grade school I was chosen to be one of a trio of boys who sang, "We Three Kings of Orient Are," but during the performance I forgot the words to my brief solo part. As a freshman at Oldham High School I began taking trombone lessons but then the basketball season started and I abandoned the trombone forever. I had practiced just enough at home, filling the house with sour sounds, so that my parents put up very little resistance to my quitting the trombone. The concert choir at Augustana Academy, where I finished high school, was as good as any high school choir in the country and I felt privileged when the respected director, Clifton Madsen, picked me to sing bass. However he placed me between the two strongest basses and insisted I take voice lessons as a condition for singing in the choir. Mr. Madsen suggested the "Lord's Prayer" as my recital piece, believing, I think, that I already knew the words and could thus concentrate fully on the notes. Since then nobody has ever seriously suggested I join a choir.

Besides loving music I appreciate its contribution to my life and the life of our church. I agree with Martin Luther when he said that, after theology, God's greatest gift to us is music. Music seems to sink into the deepest recesses of our beings better than visual or verbal stimulation. Recently I heard the old fifties song, "Lavender Blue, (Dilly, Dilly)." It put me back into the Oldham café fifty-five years ago. I could visualize the entire setting—the tables, booths and the juke box. I saw the faces and heard the voices of my friends and the owner, Gene Gruenhagen, working behind the counter. The song took me home. The great old Lenten hymns do much the same for me. They transport me back to one of the mid-week Lenten Services at Oldham Lutheran Church on an early spring evening. I am back there in the pew with my mother and brother listening to a neighboring pastor who has come as part of the round robin rotation between the churches. With the wooden pews and floor, low ceiling and hard walls we sounded like a great choir as we sang "Beneath the Cross of Jesus." Other songs and hymns carry the same magical power because music grabs us down deep and holds on.

During my seminary days I learned something about the power of music, only in a negative way. Two of the professors at Luther Theological Seminary were from Eastern Europe. They had fled from Hitler and his Third Reich armies. Even though they had been in the United States for at least ten years they were unable to sing the hymn, "Glories of Your Name Are Spoken," because the tune by Haydn was the same as the German National Anthem. Instead of visualizing the cross they saw swastikas when they heard the hymn tune. The wonderful text was not able to overcome the negative and powerful vibes of the music.

I'm afraid my colleagues have considered me to be a pest sometimes when it comes to selecting hymns for worship services. Choosing a hymn that carries the theme of a sermon is a temptation many pastors can't resist, even if nobody can sing the thing. I'll be honest; I don't like "strange" hymns. "Strange" means either they are new or they are too difficult for the congregation to sing. If a new hymn is to be introduced from time to time (preferably with long intervals in between) it should be introduced with the help of a soloist or choir and with the organist playing only the

melody line. In my last two pastorates, before retiring, I compiled a list of
110 hymns—all favorites—and made it clear I preferred we stick to the list.
There is nothing even mildly positive about a congregation struggling to
get through a forgettable hymn. Why suffer defeat so quickly after hearing
a message of victory?

The so-called "gospel hymns" are just fine. They are easier to sing, especially for the men, because they have great melodies and seem to be pitched
a little lower. True, they may slide south theologically from time to time
and be a little self-centered as opposed to God centered (subjective rather
than objective). But it is of little consequence, for purposes of congrega-
tional worship, if they don't measure up to all the definitions of a Lutheran
chorale. The colleges can sort all of that out in "Chorale 101." We come
to church to sing with gladness and gusto as we lift our praises to the Lord
with untrained and straining voices in a weekly unveiling of joyous medi-
ocrity. How could there possibly be a debate over whether a congregation
should lift the rafters with a gospel song like "Blessed Assurance" or sink
into the basement trying to survive a complicated and heavy hymn with
archival tones?

Music is a gift and those who bring it to us or help us with it are gifts
too. Over the years I have been exceedingly privileged to participate in worship with some wonderful organists. Not only were they good at the organ,
they also demonstrated patience with an unprofessional like me meddling
in their profession. I have tested them by sometimes asking them to either
slow it down or speed it up, depending on the hymn. Worse, I have on a
few occasions wondered out loud why they did not stick to the melody
instead of doing all the little variations that seem to throw a congregation
off the hymn track. Is it a rule of thumb that the larger the organ and the
more accomplished the organist the more likely it is that the congregation
will have to fight the organist somewhere during the singing of the hymn?
Perhaps we need to re-visit the meaning of the word "accompany."

The principal organist at the church where I now worship is exceptional
in so many ways. Periodically she does something unique. When she senses
the congregation has gathered up a head of steam on a hymn she quits
playing and cuts us loose to form a wonderful a cappella chorus for a verse
or two. It's her way of saying, "See, you can get along without me." Usually
at the end, before we slide too far off the melody, she comes back in and
we finish the hymn together, which is her way to remind us she is there to
help us. Her performance as an organist serves always to make us aware of
what a beautiful instrument the organ is and how suitable it is for church
music.

But the organ is not the only instrument that belongs in the church. In recent years we have introduced so-called "contemporary" services. Guitars, keyboards, flutes, drums and a host of other instruments have appeared up front. During the nineteen sixties and seventies, when I was in campus ministry, these were the instruments of choice when folk music was so much in vogue. Those of us who recall some of those wonderful folk songs would welcome new hymns with texts written for songs like "This Land is Your Land" or "Four Strong Winds." Many of the well known hymns we love to sing came from old folk songs. I have appreciated all of the fine musicians who share their talents with the congregation by playing or singing in the contemporary worship. While there are some wonderful new songs I always appreciate it when they put their energy and talent into providing accompaniment for one of the great old hymns, which, as a whole, comprise one of the great treasures of the church. Those who play in our contemporary services face a huge challenge. Many of them play in other groups where the emphasis is on performance. But, in church, we ask them to step back and see themselves not only as performers who relish "getting it on" but as servants, helping the worshippers to sing their praises too.

Speaking of performance leads me to the choir. Back in the mists of time we as a church came up with the idea that choirs should be heard and not seen. Many church choirs were seated in the rear balcony to avoid any semblance of performing. But that is what choirs do—they perform. They also help the congregation sing but the reason they practice and robe up and sit together is to perform. So, all that was accomplished was to change the place of performance from front to back. And, in the process, something was lost. An unseen choir is not very personal. Are we always sure it's the choir and not a tape recording? Not unless we venture a peek. Furthermore God works through people and people have faces and faces have expressions. I am always moved by the intensity of the conductor and the faces of the singers as they interpret the music. I do not find it distracting to watch the choir sing. On the contrary, I find it enhancing my worship as I both watch and hear the singers at the same time. Singing is a joyful act and their eyes show it. They draw me into the praises they sing.

Has anyone ever suggested the pastor preach his sermon from the back of the church? There are times I would have welcomed that in order to be less identified with the sermon I was preaching. Then I would not have had to witness the drooping eyelids out in front of me. Furthermore, the congregation would not be distracted as I frantically scan my notes for the next point or send a spray of saliva into the front row as I round out the word "Thessalonians." The idea is far-fetched, I know, but something of a logical sequence to putting the choir in the back.

Perhaps I have now achieved the status of a grumpy old man, at least among some musicians. Those who don't know me may think so. Those who do will know I like to make a point as forcefully as possible to encourage others to think and clarify their own opinions. I am eager to encourage discussion, perhaps better informed than mine.

And thank you to anyone who has ever sung for me or with me or helped me sing. We have shared the marvelous gift of music and you have opened a window through which I can send my prayers and praises to God. Abraham Lincoln was right when he said, "Listening to music, every man becomes his own poet." You have unleashed a powerful force that, more than anything else, has stirred my soul and given me a peace and joy beyond what words can express. You have transported me to my home, my Heavenly home, where those who have gone before are a part of the great choir singing songs of praise and thanksgiving. I can see their faces as they sing, sparkling with joy.

Thanks be to God for the gift of music.

Choices

I spent a couple of my high school summers working at Ne So Dak Bible Camp in northeastern South Dakota as a generalist—mowing lawns, lifeguarding, playing softball and basketball, working in the canteen, doing light maintenance and, otherwise, hanging out. My friend, Ray Engh, had worked there for several years and knew the ropes so I was his understudy, although my status was elevated by having a car, a '37 Chevy Coupe, which we took to Webster every Saturday night to buy a malted milk and watch a movie. Webster was approximately 100 rounds of "Ninety-Nine Bottles of Beer on the Wall" away from the camp, a musical feat Ray and I accomplished one Saturday night when we were in a giddy mood.

Along with all of his other skills Ray was something of a psychologist when he worked behind the counter of the canteen. Campers would come and ask what kind of ice cream we had. We sold only vanilla ice cream but Ray would answer, "Plain, White and Vanilla." A few caught on immediately but others would spend some time pondering their choices. Some wanted more information. What was the difference? Ray had an answer to further complicate the moment. Plain was "really" very plain and ordinary, Vanilla had an unmistakable vanilla flavor and White was absolutely without any color whatsoever. That seemed to make the choice even more difficult. For a couple of days, before everyone caught on, we had fun with the ruse and also got a chance to watch how difficult choices can be.

We don't require much of an example to know something about the difficulty of making choices, whether they are big or small. Recently I watched one of my granddaughters as she picked out a candy bar at a convenience store. By the time she finally settled on the item she wanted she had picked up and put back several different candy bars. During the course of her indecision I reminded her that this would not be the last candy bar of her whole life.

But I could not be too hard on her because I had once gone through the same kind of process on a slightly higher level. I had a Letter of Call to a church in the Black Hills which, for a variety of reasons, was very appealing to me. But I also dearly loved the church in Watertown where I served, and the community as well. I carried on a lively and frustrating debate with myself, first marshalling arguments for staying and then listing arguments for going. Neither list seemed to topple the other. I prayed for guidance, asking for some kind of sign that even a non-mystic like myself could understand. I sought counsel from trusted friends. Finally I wrote two letters, one of acceptance and one of refusal. I had them both with me as I drove to the Post Office but when I got to the mail drop I continued driving. I drove out into the country and wandered around on the gravel roads of Codington County, trying to make a decision. Finally I went home with both letters on the front seat.

Later, on Saturday night, I telephoned the chair of the call committee and said I would come and told him they could announce it on Sunday morning. Then I went down to the basement and wept. After a sleepless night I called them back early Sunday morning and told them I had changed my mind. In the meantime I had resigned my position in Watertown at the Saturday service, making it necessary to also reverse myself at home on Sunday morning. Somehow word reached the folks in the Black Hills that I was having second thoughts, so they returned the Letter of Call and I entered a second cycle of indecision, just as difficult as the first. Having made the same decision the second time, I had the dubious privilege of receiving the call a third time but by then I had formed the habit of saying "no" and the process was easier. All in all, it was a very wobbly time and I was somewhat shocked by my indecisiveness and my emotional instability. Being pulled in opposite directions by two equally powerful forces is not a situation I would wish on any one. I have discovered that some decisions are incredibly hard for me to make, and I admire those who have the ability to be decisive and firm, never looking back once they have made their choice.

I had a coach who regularly delivered a stock assessment whenever things seemed to be going in a direction not intended. "Oh well," he would say, "It won't change the price of peanuts in China." Applying that bit of folk wisdom to the choices we make might help us to see that life will go on just fine, regardless of how we choose, so long as we are determined to follow up on our choices. My granddaughter's choice of a candy bar was right because she was determined to enjoy the one she selected. My decision (or lack of it!) worked out fine because I was determined to make it work. The Black Hills congregation found a very fine pastor, and I had some more good years in Watertown.

Some choices may cause us to take ourselves too seriously, as though the fate of the world depends on us. Really we are not much more than a grain of sand on the beach in the total scheme of things. Other choices may cause us to take ourselves too lightly, as though we don't have the ability to make either choice work. As long as both choices are good, even right, one can't loose for winning and God will watch over us and bless us and our work as always.

So far I have not gone beyond culinary and vocational choices. There is another choice about which one cannot be quite so cavalier. That would be the most important choice a person makes in life.

Joshua had such a choice in mind when he gathered the tribes of Israel together at Shechem to renew the Covenant God had originally made with Abraham. Joshua had successfully led the Hebrew people in battle as they attempted to conquer the land which God had promised to give them. But settling the new land presented another challenge. With no experience in agriculture they were now under the gun to make a success of raising crops and developing herds. Those who had lived there before, Canaanites and others, had developed a fertility cult centered around the god, Baal. When sufficiently placated, they believed, Baal would cause their land to produce and their herds to reproduce. The Hebrew people had no agricultural colleges or extension agents to help them become agriculturists. Why not seek Baal's help then? The temptation was great and Joshua believed the consequences were enormous. In an effort to remind the people who it was that had brought them to this place and to strengthen their allegiance to God Joshua spoke in a forceful and personal way to the assembly at Shechem.

> "Now, therefore revere the Lord, and serve him in sincerity and in faithfulness; put away the gods that your ancestors served beyond the River and in Egypt, and serve the Lord. Now if you are unwilling to serve the Lord, choose

this day whom you will serve, . . . but as for me and my household, we will serve the Lord." (Joshua 24:14,15)

"Choose" is not a word that is used much in the Gospels. But the concept is certainly there. When Jesus invited people to come to him so that they might find rest, he was asking people to choose him. By describing himself as "The Way" he beckoned people to believe in him. As he sat on the hillside, brooding over the waywardness of those who lived in Jerusalem and recalling how unwilling they had been to heed his call, he regretted their poor choice.

Nor does the word "choose" appear often in The Acts of the Apostles where you might expect to see it, given the missionary stories one finds there. But the idea is in, with and under each chapter as Peter and Paul proclaim the good news of the Risen Lord. One example will suffice. Paul and Silas had been thrown into a prison in Philippi because they were, as usual, turning things upside down. They sat up late, making holy hoopla together, praying and singing until midnight, when there was a violent earthquake. All the doors of the jail swung open and the jailer feared that Paul and Silas, among others, had escaped. The jailer was about to take his life when Paul shouted loudly, "We're all here." So moved was the jailer by the example of Paul and Silas that he wanted the courage and faith they had. How could he be saved? "Believe on the Lord Jesus," they answered. The jailer washed their wounds and invited Paul and Silas to talk to his family. They believed and he and his family were baptized "without delay." The jailer had chosen well. (Acts 16:25-34)

When the word "choose" does appear in the New Testament it usually refers to God's action. "You did not choose me," said Jesus, "but I chose you." (John 15:16) God's people are described as a "chosen race" as a way to describe God's initiative in the story of faith and God's possessing love. (I Peter 2:9) What mystery there is in the idea of God, the creator of the universe, choosing to show his hand for all the world to see. That would have to be described as the best of all choices.

Jesus

Who was Jesus?

I can't tell you how many times I have read the Bible, some portions more often than others. I have no idea how often I have gone to church. I could not begin to list the articles on religion, theological books, Biblical commentaries or Christian devotionals I have read. I wonder how many religious classes I have taught over the years. The answer to all of these questions would be "lots!"

But, somehow, I think all of these activities take a back seat to dealing with the question of "Who was Jesus?" Whether one is a high powered theologian with an impressive array of academic credentials or an everyday Christian plumber dealing primarily with the problems of getting water either into or out of a building, the question, "Who was Jesus?" is at the very center of personal faith. Every other Christian teaching or thought revolves around Jesus like so many circles around a bull's eye on a target.

In 1949 the British historian, Herbert Butterfield, wrote a book with the title, *Christianity and History*, in which he traced the role of Christianity throughout history. At the end of his book he faced the future with the uncertainty of one who is more accustomed to musing about what has happened than what might happen, more as a historian than a philosopher. But his conclusion amounted to a ringing call to hold to the center.

"We can do worse than remember a principle which both gives us a firm Rock and leaves us the maximum elasticity for our minds: the principle: Hold to Christ, and for the rest be totally uncommitted."

We know where an attempt to answer the question, "Who was Jesus?" will lead, even as we begin. It will lead us into a divine mystery where our language and categories gradually disappear beyond our ability to follow. And, in the end, that will be a welcome experience for we will by then have realized that to "pin Jesus down," so to speak, is not something we either want or need. It is good to know that he is beyond our comprehension and that somehow we are more satisfied with mystery than with clarity.

But that does not mean we should not try to arrive at a clearer picture and a better understanding of Jesus than we may now have. The author of John's Gospel believed the more we knew of Jesus the more likely we might be receptive to the gift of faith. He, like the other gospel writers, recorded the words and deeds of Jesus "so that you may come to believe that Jesus is the Messiah, the Son of God, and that through believing you may have life in his name." (John 20: 31)

When Luther noted how dismal the level of Christian understanding was among the people in the church of his day he launched an effort to make the home a place of instruction. In 1525 Luther wrote his *Small Catechism* in simple question and answer form. As parents instructed their children, they, too, might learn the basics of the Christian Faith. Luther included the Lord's Prayer, Ten Commandments, Apostles' Creed, Baptism, the Lord's Supper and Confession (The Power of the Keys). The simple and profound explanations Luther provided are generally regarded as classic statements of Christian theology, particularly those interpreting the Apostles' Creed.

In his explanation to the Second Article of the Apostles' Creed Luther wrote, "I believe that Jesus Christ, true God, Son of the Father from eternity . . . is my Lord."

Jesus brings something with him that no other great or good human being could, namely a sampling of eternity. Scripture tells us that Jesus was without sin, which immediately sets him apart from any other human being. Moreover, Jesus was eminently qualified to deal with this world's problems since he had been in on its creation. Could there possibly be anyone better suited to fixing one's automobile than the person who designed and manufactured it?

Given the divinity of Jesus, one wonders how important God's selection of human parents actually was. What little we know of Mary and

Joseph suggests they were model parents. But, as God, Jesus had a built in resistance to all negative forces and so could possibly have been raised by almost anyone with no serious consequences. Recognizing the divine nature of Jesus helps us to see that God was not going to leave much to chance. Salvation was too important an enterprise to place in the hands of one of us, no matter how wonderful a specimen of humanity could be found.

There have been some in the history of the church who have found it impossible to believe that a divine Jesus could become a man in any real sense. The earliest proponents of this "heresy" were the Gnostics who denied the possibility of mixing the divine and human any more than one can mix oil and water. They believed that the visible, historical Jesus was an apparition, a phantom merely appearing to be human. In one form or another this point of view is still with us and we all must contend with the impulse to hold on to the divinity of Jesus to the exclusion of his humanity. He was also a man.

In his explanation to the Second Article of the Apostles' Creed Luther goes on to say, "I believe that Jesus Christ, true man, born of the Virgin Mary is my Lord." The key word is "born." Now the role of Mary and Joseph takes on enormous importance. Since Jesus was born to them he also had to be raised in their home. As the "Mother of God" Mary deserves more attention than most Protestants have given to her. She "mothered" Jesus as he grew and developed into a young man, teaching him to pray, molding and shaping his intellectual, social and spiritual character and modeling the godly life. Her role in the life and teaching of Jesus cannot be overstated. Nor can Joseph's, whose rough carpenter's hands steadied Jesus as he learned to walk or gripped the board as Jesus made his first cuts with a saw.

Scripture declares that Jesus was human and that he was tempted in the same way all humans are tempted, yet he was without sin. In his 1955 novel, *The Last Temptation of Christ*, Nikos Kazantzakis portrays Jesus struggling in the last, excruciating moments of his life with sexual thoughts about Mary Magdalene. Before he dies he is able to overcome the temptation and find peace in his faithfulness to God's purpose. To the extent we have denied the humanity of Jesus, we find it shocking to imagine Jesus entertaining sexual fantasies or any other kind of troubling temptation. But it is not inconsistent with Scripture.

Just as the Gnostics denied the humanity of Jesus there have also been heresies in Christian history that have denied his divinity. Early on the "Monarchians" declared that Jesus was a man, and nothing more, but one on whom the Holy Spirit had descended so powerfully that he was endowed with great spiritual insight and energy. Many, who have little taste for the miraculous, have found the Monarchian reasoning to be attractive. For example, Thomas Jefferson compiled what is referred to as *Jefferson's Bible*, in which he excised all references to the supernatural and focused, instead, on the teaching of Jesus. Jefferson took Jesus as a great teacher and a great man, but not God.

But C.S. Lewis, in *Mere Christianity*, has forever put an end to any attempt to accept Jesus as a great teacher and, at the same time, reject his claim to be God. Any moral teacher who said the things that Jesus said would not be either very moral or a good teacher. Either Jesus was what he said he was or he was some kind of madman, even a devil. When Jesus said, "I and the Father are one," it was either true or the ranting of a megalomaniac. We can't have it both ways.

Who was Jesus? According to Luther and classical Christianity he was both God and man, divine and human. Holding on to that central truth has not been easy, either for the church or individuals. Many councils of the church were called and most of the creeds were written to clarify who Jesus was in order to help the church steer clear of those who would pick one side or the other. Jesus was not just God. Jesus was not just man. Jesus was both.

Martin Luther has also helped us understand the importance of paradoxical thinking when it comes to holding a great truth together. A paradox is a way to reconcile two seemingly opposite concepts. For example, we say that "absence makes the heart grow fonder." But we also say, "out of sight, out of mind." While those two observations (maxims) are both true, they are also diametrically opposed to each other. When it comes to explaining the complexities of human relationships we are forced to admit what is true is so large that it needs to be bracketed rather than narrowly defined. One idea is true, its opposite is true and everything in between is true. So the answer to the question, "Was Jesus divine or human?" is "yes!"

It is interesting to stand back and reflect on our own experience to see how we slide back and forth on the spectrum created by the divine-human paradox.

When we sing "What a Friend We Have in Jesus" we think of the human Jesus. But when we sing "Oh, Worship the King" we have in mind the divine Jesus.

When we note that Jesus had to be awakened from his sleep out there in the boat, weary as he was from the press of the crowds, we understand how it was for Jesus the human. And when we watch Jesus calm the storm at sea we feel we have witnessed the power of God in Jesus.

When we see Jesus standing outside of Lazarus' tomb, weeping out of a personal sense of loss and because he felt sorry for Lazarus' sisters, Mary and Martha, we feel a kinship with Jesus, the man. But when Jesus commands Lazarus to rise up and come out of the tomb we know we are in the presence of God.

When Jesus sat by the well and asked the Samaritan woman for a drink, we can understand how drained and dependent he was at that moment. In our thirst we have relied on others for a drink. That was a human moment. But when Jesus tells her that he could give her a drink of living water that would assuage her thirst forever we know it is God speaking.

When Jesus hung in agony on the cross and cried out "My God, why have you forsaken me?" we understand all too well that human sense of loneliness and abandonment. But then Jesus told the repentant thief, "Today you will be with me in paradise," and we know it is only God who can open the gates of heaven. We are reminded of his promise of eternal life to all who believe—a divine promise if there ever was one.

Who was Jesus? He was the Son of God. He was the Son of Man. More important for us he is the Savior. We will never in a lifetime be able to wrap our arms intellectually around Jesus. He is too large, too wonderful and too mysterious for that. But, in the long run, we are absolutely delighted to know that he has wrapped his arms around us.

Rest

I have always regarded rest as something more than seven hours of sleep at night even though I think that is what a local television newscaster had in mind when he closed his nighttime broadcast years ago with the signature statement: "Rest easy." That, after sometimes delivering news guaranteed to keep one awake. Since, in the well known creation story from Genesis, God himself rested after a six day creation effort, it may be well to explore some of the dimensions of rest.

The first Bible Camp I attended was held at Ne So Dak Bible Camp on the shores of Lake Enemy Swim in northeastern South Dakota. Summer camp plunged us into a whole new environment where the routine of home was replaced with a brand new schedule. It meant getting up earlier than usual (for those of us from town, at least), attending sessions in the morning and evening, swimming for a good chunk of the afternoon and finding sleep elusive in a cabin full of boys. All of this was accompanied with the stress of some homesickness and the awkwardness of trying to make and keep new friends. In an attempt to keep us from becoming totally frayed the camp scheduled a quiet hour from one to two in the afternoon. For the most part we observed this forced lull in our daily routine, especially when our counselor was in the room. If we did not sleep at least we remained more or less horizontal for the better part of the hour. Thus total exhaustion and maybe illness was staved off. Left to ourselves we likely would have kept up our frenetic pace, only to be delivered home at the end of the week limp and spent, having absorbed little of the "Bible" part of the camp. Sometimes, it would seem, we need to be told to get some rest because adults, too, get caught up in the busyness and stresses of life and neglect this basic need and either harm themselves or fail to get the most out of life.

When I was a seminary student, married and with one child, money was in short supply even though my wife worked as a nurse in a Minneapolis hospital. During the Christmas season I attempted to supplement our income by getting a job at Dayton's, a large department store on Nicollet Avenue in downtown Minneapolis. I would like to say my part-time job consisted of selling sweaters, canoes or some other sought-after products where my persuasive abilities could be tested. But I was not entrusted with that kind of responsibility. Instead I wandered throughout the multi-storied store with a broom and a long handled dust pan sweeping up cigarette butts. I think my folks were mildly embarrassed by the inglorious depths to which their son, a college graduate, had sunk. Those were the days when people smoked everywhere, even as they leisurely shopped throughout Dayton's. I smoked a pipe at the time so I would occasionally slip into one of the many employee lounges for a smoke. In one of those rooms the Santa Clauses would gather, donning their red and white outfits, strapping on their beards, changing shifts, swapping stories and smoking cigarettes. The poor fellows had to keep their jolly faces on for hours at a time when they were out in the store but, in the back room, they could be themselves, which for them was a form of rest. Rest is like that, relaxing in the company of others where there is no need to pretend or be "on duty." Rest, of this sort, is a welcome respite for those who must wear a public face, whether that rest is found at home or around a table at a favorite hangout with friends.

When I was little we would often travel to my grandparents' farm, nestled in the rolling hills west of Garretson. I have a bundle of memories from those days. One particularly applies to the topic of rest and it is as vivid as any memory I have. It was nap time. My father accompanied me up to the south room where I lay down in the bed reserved for my brother and me. The curtains gently billowed as the summer breeze slipped through the open window. The bed was up against the north wall of the bedroom and, once I lay down, my father flopped down on the outer edge. I lay between the wall and him, luxuriating in a feeling of total security. I was protected and I was safe, nestling, cocoon like, in complete shelter. His succumbing to quick sleep and labored snoring only enhanced my sense of being protected by one stronger than I. Is not such a sense of security a necessary ingredient for complete rest, I wonder, not only for children but really for anyone? Even in a world filled with accidents and illness, somewhere down deep it is restful to know we are ultimately safe.

Of all the jabs a pastor receives the most favored by wags is that he works only one day a week. I always disagreed. "No, you are wrong," I protested, "we work only half a day." My purpose now is not to defend my profession except to say that by Sunday afternoon I was usually exhausted. Sometimes that would lead to a nap, usually as a golf match played out on TV. I assumed the reason the commentators spoke in whispered tones was so they would not keep me from dozing or, once asleep, wake me up. More often than not I would find rest by doing something physical, in contrast to the mental exertion of the prior week which culminated in preaching four weekend sermons. I was brought up to not work on Sundays but I have amended that rule to allow work I find restful. Mowing or watering the lawn becomes a welcome form of relaxation. Or maybe a twenty-five mile bike ride. Or fishing or hunting. Or, as a last resort, golf! Vigorous activity is restful because it is renewing, partly because finally one is now alone with himself to think his own thoughts and sweat out a few frustrations and also because it will lead to a sounder sleep at night.

For nearly forty years I have hunted turkeys in the Black Hills. The season is in the spring and serves as an antidote to whatever cabin fever we have experienced during the winter. The Black Hills are particularly beautiful in April. Generally there is a little residue of snow on the north side of the mountains but pasque flowers are blooming on the south side. There is a freshness filling the air which mountain bluebirds punctuate with flashes of indigo. We get up early enough to get out into the forest before daylight and then spend a good share of the day tromping up and down the hills. After lunch we often find a sunny and sheltered spot where we can flop down for a short nap. Even though the day may be a little cool or windy the sun warms us into a tranquil slumber. It is a moment we have anticipated during a busy Lenten schedule and has become a part of the joy of Easter. We drive 450 miles to hunt turkeys and to take a blissful nap under the pines. The turkeys always remain elusive; the nap is a constant. I have always wondered if slumber is more complete in, say, the Lincoln bedroom at the White House or under a canopied bed in a luxurious old castle than it is in my own bed. I doubt it. But out there in the Black Hills on a soft spring day and on the hard ground, tired from hiking and warmed by the sun, I think I sleep a quality sleep. The setting is right as the cares of the world slide away.

Sometimes, even though the situation is not suitable, we seek rest because it is absolutely necessary. After my sophomore year at Augustana Academy some of us lingered long enough to find a summer job building an elevator. Huge cement towers would rise above Canton that summer as work continued around the clock. We applied at the makeshift office late one afternoon, and we were immediately hired to work the night shift. So without any sleep we came to work. We were assigned the task of unloading bags of cement from a box car. Each bag weighed ninety-four pounds, and we were soft after nine months of school but we went about the task industriously. It did not take long before we were exhausted. We allowed ourselves a break which was quickly broken by a sharp scolding from our boss. He used language that reminded us we were no longer in the classroom. An experience like that may be one of the ways a sixteen year old becomes more worldly wise. Not only did we survive the barrage of invectives but we also learned to slow down and rest a little as we worked, straightening up and catching our breath between bags. We worked there all summer, eventually being assigned easier tasks and becoming tougher as the days went by. Sometimes one can make intervals of rest even while doing tough duty.

I have probably not scratched the surface when it comes to studying the subject of rest. Each of us would have our favorite stories of how we have experienced rest, or how it has eluded us. We commonly think of rest as a physical experience but it is an important spiritual concept too. A brief look at the stories I have told and their application may tie some loose ends together.

The third commandment instructs us to keep the Sabbath: "Remember the Sabbath Day to keep it holy." The Sabbath honors the God who created the world even as it recalls that he rested from his work. Like all the other commandments, it is given for our benefit. God knows that we need rest, and he does not leave it up to us to figure that out. Much like the forced quiet hour at Bible Camp God commands that we rest for our own good.

The kind of rest God commands includes coming into his presence to hear and learn his word. It is a "come as you are" invitation. Like Santa Claus on a break we can let down and be ourselves. As the beloved hymn, "Rock of Ages," puts it: "Nothing in my hands I bring, simply to thy cross I cling." Not only is it restful to not have to pretend that we are more than we are, it is also restful to realize God accepts us just as we are.

To rest in God is to experience absolute security, sheltered in God's care. "Let me hide myself in Thee" is the Christian's version of snuggling up next to a parent in bed. To rest is to relax in God and to know we are safe, even amidst the dangers of this world. Nothing, including death, can separate us from God's grip on us.

Rest, as God provides it, does not mean inactivity. Work that is satisfying and fulfilling is restful because it generates renewal even while we do it. Doing work that we know is pleasing to God, whether it is our job or volunteer work, is like a good bike ride or hike. We complete the task tired but refreshed and grateful for the experience.

Sometimes life is so good we just want to flop down on the ground and soak up the sunshine of his grace. We are struck by the beauty of the earth and sky and thankful he has given us the capacity to enjoy his whole creation. Rest comes from knowing we are at one with God and his creation.

With God's help we find ways to achieve rest even while we struggle with life's challenges. Many have found prayer to be helpful in fighting off spiritual exhaustion. I am not thinking now of formal, carefully written prayers but prayers of a sentence or less. We slow down, straighten our backs, breathe in deeply and utter a phrase to God even as we lift that next bag of cement. Our prayer may include such words as "help," "bless," "thanks," "keep," or "forgive." God knows. God will fill in the gaps.

St. Augustine is credited with praying, "Oh Lord, our souls are restless until they find rest in Thee." Exhaustion comes to us on many levels and so there are many levels of rest, bordered by a good night's rest on the physical side and a good God's generous gift of grace on the spiritual side. "Rest easy."

Bells

The English poet, John Donne, is perhaps best known today for a series of meditations called *Devotions Upon Emergent Occasions*, written in 1624. One of these contains an eloquent passage which begins, "Who bends not his ear to any bell which upon any occasion rings?"

Bells do have a way of making us perk up our ears. As I think back over the years it is interesting to recall the part bells have played.

My paternal grandfather became quite demanding towards the end of his life. He had been a very independent person but in his latter days had to depend on others to help him in a variety of ways. This frustrated him. He had a little bell which sat on the table near his bed, much like the bells that sit on counters for people to ring if there is no one around to serve them. When he needed assistance he wanted it right now! If he had to ring the bell a second or third time he would slam his hand down on it repeatedly. He was not to be ignored. The house would resonate with the sound of that little bell as he pushed it almost beyond its limits. People would rush to his side not so much to help him as to get him to quit pounding on the bell. I still hate to ring one of those little bells because I fear I will sound perturbed. The bell's tinkle sounds more thunderous to me than it really is. My call for help may sound too urgent. "Who bends not his ear to any bell...?"

In my hometown of Oldham we had no sirens to sound a fire alarm. Instead the person who reached the town hall first would ring a bell in a series of three rings. Instantly the town would be mobilized, the firemen racing to the town hall or to the scene of the fire while the rest of us chased the fire engine. To this day I have to check a natural instinct to follow a fire truck. It was fascinating to see how the ringing of a single bell could arouse an entire community. It caused our juices to flow as much as a wailing siren. "Who bends not his ear to any bell...?"

Bells were a strong part of my church life when I was young. On Sunday mornings the bell of our church was rung twice, one half hour before the church service started and at the beginning of the service. I'm afraid the beauty of the bell was somewhat lost on us though. Mother faced a serious challenge each Sunday morning when she called us to get up and get ready for church. Usually there was not much activity until the first bell sounded. After that it was frantic around the house. Since my father was the pastor we did not really have a half hour after the first bell. He had to be there at least ten minutes early. Fortunately we lived only four short blocks away from the church. Mother thought a good breakfast was more important than good grooming so we would often arrive in a somewhat disheveled condition, but in time to hear the second bell ring from our pew. "Who bends not his ear to any bell...?"

Other than Sunday morning the church bell marked important, transitional moments. On New Year's Eve the bell was rung to signal the passing of the old year and the arrival of the new. By then we would have had our fill of oyster stew and finished the Watch Night Service. Never was timing so critical. Normally our services were over when they were over but on New Year's Eve the service had to conclude at exactly the right time, straight up at midnight. I would sit there with one eye on my watch, wondering if the hymn or prayer would be long enough to stretch the service to midnight. Or maybe either would go too long, lingering on into the New Year. Because of poor timing would we have to sit in awkward silence before the bell could be rung? Or would we go overtime and miss the magic moment? How bush league would that be, I thought—to ring the bell five minutes into the New Year? I held my father accountable since he was the pastor whose job also included being the timekeeper this last night of the year. "Who bends not his ear to any bell...?"

Sometimes our church bell sounded a more sobering kind of transition, marking someone's passage from this world to the next. As the pall bearers carried the casket out of the church following a funeral the bell tolled a somber and measured cadence, capturing the heaviness of the moment.

One funeral, in particular, stands out in my memory. I must have been about ten years old at the time. Two boys from our church, Donald and Richard, attended a youth convention in Milwaukee. Donald had stopped by our house to visit with my mother before going to the convention. He talked with me and showed my mother the pocket his mother had sewn on his baseball uniform so that he could carry his New Testament as he played. Those who joined the Pocket Testament League promised to carry their New Testaments with them and Donald went the extra mile. A few days later during the early evening the telephone rang at our house. My father answered and it soon became evident there was dreadful news. Donald had drowned in a Milwaukee swimming pool. My father faced the difficult task of driving out to Donald's farm to tell his parents about the tragic death of their son.

I happened to be outside on the day of Donald's funeral and remember hearing the bell that marked the conclusion of the service. From our yard on the edge of town I watched the procession of hearse and cars heading west out to the cemetery. The bell continued tolling while the large crowd filed out of the church. It was overwhelming to realize death could come so quickly and deprive us all of someone so young and likeable. Death had taken Donald and also a part of us. Years later I encountered the poem by John Donne to which I have already alluded: *Devotions Upon Emergent Occasions.* Donne writes, "…any man's death diminishes me, because I am involved in mankind, and therefore never send to know for whom the bell tolls; it tolls for thee." On that day the bell tolled for Donald and for all of us. "Who bends not his ear to any bell…?"

It has been my privilege to help bring two hand bell choirs into existence at the last two churches I served before I retired. I was amazed to discover how quickly those choirs developed, usually anchored by people with considerable musical skills. Within a short time at each church we needed more bells, another "octave" was the term, so that the choirs could perform more difficult music. The bell choirs added a whole new dimension to our worship, providing a clear and lucid sound that resonated throughout the sanctuary.

Hand bells originated in England as a miniature and indoor version of the bells in the towers of churches. The bell towers often contained a "ring of bells," some with more than a dozen. Teams of ringers pulled on the ropes as they rang the bells in various combinations. It was hard and often cold work and sometimes their practicing disturbed the neighbors. Seeking greater comfort and trying to be more "neighborly," the ringers decided to gather inside around a table and practice their combinations with small bells that had leather or wooden handgrips. Eventually, as bell foundries cast a greater variety of hand bells, the ringers moved out of the church and sometimes rang carols, hymns and folk songs on the street at special times of the year.

P. T. Barnum, the great American showman, is credited with popularizing hand bells in America. In the 1840s he brought a group of English ringers to this country for an American tour. He dressed them in Swiss costumes and promoted them as "Swiss Bell Ringers." Around 1900, hand bells were introduced in New England for practice by the bell tower ringers of Old North Church of Boston. The bells, one might say, had found a church home in America. And they have never left. The hand bells' journey from England to America was acknowledged when, in 1954, the American Guild of English Hand Bell Ringers was organized.

Hand bells are cast in foundries of "bell metal," which is an alloy or mixture of about 80 percent copper and 20 percent tin. The metal is melted in a furnace at about 2000 degrees F. and then poured into molds to cool and harden. That accomplished, the bell is taken out of the mold and cleaned, polished and tuned. Extremes of heat or cold do not affect the pitch of hand bells and they never have to be tuned again, a fact not lost on church treasurers who usually regard the cost of tuning pianos and organs as excessive.

If I had to single out one word to describe the role of bells I would use the word "summon." Bells are used to summon help, to call people to lift their hearts in worship and to invite us to ponder the meaning of the moment as we observe our transitions, whether from one classroom to the next, one year to the next or this life to the next. With a clarity and simplicity unmatched by the human voice or any other instrument, a ringing bell exudes purity. A single, unwavering note skips upon the airwaves, followed by another and another. Bells, in fact, have given birth to one of the most captivating of all metaphors: "Let freedom ring."

John Donne was right when he asked the question, "Who bends not his ear to any bell which upon any occasion rings?"

Unlocked

My first parish was in Fowler, a small town in southern Colorado, along the Arkansas River. Farms, by most standards, were small in the valley where operators irrigated their land. Above the valley to the north the land opened up to vast expanses of "dry-land" farming. When it rained the farms produced abundantly, but if it did not rain, which was the case much too often, all the moisture saving techniques in the world could not salvage the crops. It was a form of living on the edge, where rewards and hazards approached the extreme. Shortly before I arrived one of the families of the congregation had lost a child to a rattlesnake bite.

It was the country stretching off to the south that held the most fascination for me. I called it "Zane Grey" country, where cattle roamed freely amidst the cedars and canyons and through the normally dry river beds. My friend, Arnold Guthals, loved everything about it. When he died prematurely in an automobile accident, most of the floral display at his funeral consisted of cedar boughs. He and I would jump into his Ford pickup and head south, down to the Apishapa River. He knew where to drive across the river, which was no great trick since it was dry most of the summer. In the spring it could be very dangerous if there was a quick melting of snow in the mountains. It had a history of flash floods, and there were some wild tales about those sudden currents that Arnold loved to relate—and maybe even embellish.

We would park the truck and take long hikes in that country. I enjoyed those walks because of the scenery and also because it was fun to watch how Arnold savored those outings. He was in his element. On one of our adventures we explored an area where Indians had drawn pictures on cave walls. Somewhere, in one of my slide files, I still have the pictures we took of those ancient pictographs forty five-years ago. Later, I accompanied the local "expert" back to the site for a more complete interpretation of those primitive symbols.

Another time Arnold brought me to an isolated cabin, sometimes used by those who worked the cattle or sheep far from any of the ranches. It was their home for stretches of time. The door was unlocked, and we went inside. The cabin was simple but clean. There were cans of food in the cupboard. Finding enough mesquite to burn in the wood burning stove would not have been a problem. It was scattered across the landscape all around the cabin. One could have survived there in any season. I found it strange that the door was not locked, a view reinforced by our having moved to Fowler from an apartment in downtown Minneapolis, where we lived during a portion of my seminary days. Arnold explained to me that it was the unwritten "law of the west" to leave such places as this unlocked. Particularly in former days, when transportation was more primitive and there might be someone coming through who would need shelter or sustenance. A person caught on the wrong side of a rising river or in a storm could bide his time in the cabin. If one was lost or had miles to travel there would be the comfort of a roof, a can of beans, a bed and a wood burning fire. A sequel to the "law of the west" was to leave the cabin the way one found it, minus, maybe, a can of beans.

Jesus, too, advocated a kind of spiritual "law of the west." He bristled whenever he encountered hearts that were locked against the entrance of others. Once a lawyer tried to test Jesus by asking him, "Teacher, what must I do to inherit eternal life?" Jesus referred him to the law, which, of course, the lawyer knew well and was proud to recite. "You shall love the Lord your God with all your heart, and with all your soul, and with all your strength, and with all your mind," the lawyer answered. "And," he concluded, "your neighbor as yourself." When Jesus commended him on getting it right the lawyer tried to trip Jesus up on a technicality. Just who was his neighbor, the lawyer countered.

So Jesus told the familiar story of the "Good Samaritan." (Luke 10:25-37) There was a man, said Jesus, traveling on one of the most dangerous roads in the region, winding downward from Jerusalem to Jericho, when he was accosted by highwaymen. They beat him up, took everything he had, including his clothes, and left him half dead. Later a man of the cloth, a priest, appeared, but instead of rushing to help the victim he crossed the road to the other side and walked past. Similarly, a Levite, whose primary interest was religion, came by and saw the victim sprawled along the edge of the road. He, too, drifted to the other side of the road and hurried on.

Jesus chose two persons who clearly knew it was their duty to help someone in need. Had they been average run-of-the-mill tourists, with light ethical standards and not wishing to have their vacations disturbed by a bloody rescue, they might have been excused. But not these two; they knew better. Jesus made a point of describing how they both shifted over to the other side of the road. Could they not stand the sight of blood? Or, more likely, were they trying to de-personalize the moment? Failing to see the man clearly may have been their way of escaping their obligation. We do find it easier to ignore the pleas of those whom we can't see. Bending over and looking the man in the eyes may have been enough to tug at their hearts, something they wanted to avoid. Or maybe they were both running late for a theological conference where they were first up to present papers on the theme of "Love." It was important to be on time.

Whatever the reason for shirking their duty, Jesus clearly implies they missed their calling at that moment. But then Jesus describes the third passerby. He was a Samaritan, with a standing among the Jews roughly equivalent to one whom we suspect today as having terrorist sympathies. Ethnic, religious and cultural barriers separated him from the Jews. Yet, moved with pity, this man stops, administers first aid, places the injured man on his animal and takes him to an inn, where he continues to care for him throughout the day. The next day, when he must leave, the Samaritan pays the innkeeper to keep and care for the patient and promises to pay more if his payment comes up short.

When Jesus asks the lawyer to tell him who the real neighbor was, his answer is not forthright. He could not say the dreaded word, "It was the *Samaritan.*" Instead, he softened his answer: "The one who showed him mercy." By then Jesus had made his point. Our neighbor is anyone and everyone in need. And, by implication, Jesus made the point that our hearts should be unlocked in order to provide warmth, sustenance and shelter to anyone whom we know to be in need. It was not exactly the "law of the west," but it was God's law and it sought to accomplish a similar outcome—"You shall love your neighbor as yourself." Most of us have a warm spot in our hearts for those who are close to us. We would be right there, ready to help, should they need us. But as the circle of people widens beyond the scope of those we know and see, we are inclined to lock up our hearts in order to shut out the strangers. Jesus preferred the word "friend" to "stranger." Throughout his ministry he reminded us that only by unlocking our hearts, so that others may enter, will we be able to substitute the word "friend" for "stranger."

Knowing Grace

The cattle tank stood to the south and below the windmill on my grand-father's farm. It was a large tank made of oak. Over the years the cattle and horses had worn a hollow around the tank from standing and kicking the ground in an effort to shake off the flies, causing the tank to look as though it was built on a pedestal. Every morning in the summer my grand-father would go down to the windmill to release the brake and open the windmill. Seventy feet in the air, the windmill caught the currents coming over the grove to the north. Its rudder swung into the wind, the vanes began to twirl and the shaft reaching down into the well began to pump the sweet water from two hundred feet below the surface. The pure and sparkling water poured into the cattle tank, usually spilling over the top before my grandfather remembered to close the windmill. The water was as clear and cold as a mountain stream.

But, as the day wore on into late afternoon, the cattle tank began to change. By then the cows and horses would have come to drink their fill, making the trip several times on a hot day. As the day wore on some of the water evaporated from the summer wind and, since it was an old tank, some water seeped out around the bottom. As the water level dropped and the water warmed, great globs of green algae formed on the surface, creating a forbidding appearance. Neither man nor beast found it appeal-ing anymore. The cattle gathered around the water covered with the slimy moss and bellowed their protests like college students complaining about the cafeteria.

If my grandfather was out in the hayfield the cattle had to put up with their sorry lot. He never permitted me to turn the windmill on or off. But when he returned he would open the windmill and soon the tank would be filled and the green slime would slip out over the rim of the tank. Once again the cattle tank sparkled with clean, cold water and the cows and horses drank their fill. And so it went, day after day.

When Nicodemus slipped through the darkness of the night to see Jesus he came with questions. Little is said of his motivation to meet Jesus but we can surmise he came with a thirsty heart. Apparently he came on his own rather than as an emissary of the Pharisees, of which he was one. Had he been delegated to make inquiry of Jesus he would more than likely have gone in the light of day. Nicodemus came as a listener. "We know," he said "that you are a teacher who has come from God; for no one can do these signs that you do apart from the presence of God." (John 3:2) No accusations, no arguments, no confrontation. Rather, Nicodemus acknowledged an observation, presumably shared by others, that was really an invitation for Jesus to pick it up from there. And pick it up Jesus did.

Was Nicodemus looking for greater wisdom, more answers or a new teaching? Was he on a philosophical quest? Nothing like that would fill the tank and clear off the sludge in his heart. Jesus detected that Nicodemus came with a dry heart and went right to the point. "Very truly, I tell you," Jesus told him, "no one can see the kingdom of God without being born from above." (John 3:3) As he had traveled to Jesus, Nicodemus may have pondered many possibilities of what Jesus might say. This was not one of them. "Born from above," "born anew,"—what was that all about? As it turned out, it was all about grace.

As a Pharisee, Nicodemus was a striver, meticulously keeping the law and tirelessly doing good works. That was how one pleased God and secured an eternal future. He would have made a good neighbor, the kind you leave the keys to your house with when you go away. When he blew the snow out of his driveway he, more likely than not, would have done yours too. He could have taken the Sunday offering home and counted alone without raising any eyebrows. But his tank was low. The goodness he achieved by keeping the law was not filling his heart. He was like a beautiful bird that couldn't fly. He was like a cattle tank from which others had drunk and where there had been evaporation and seepage. Moss was forming at the edges and curling toward the center. Tepid and low in spirit, he was open to a breakthrough.

Nicodemus had never been swept off his feet before. His feet were too firmly planted on the Law. So Jesus tells Nicodemus that instead of being a striver he needs to become a receiver. Could that point be any more forcefully made than by using the metaphor of new birth? We have absolutely nothing to do with our birth. It is a gift. Birth happens to us! And so, too, does grace. Grace happens!

And now here was Jesus talking about water and wind and a second birth: "Very truly, I tell you, no one can enter the kingdom of God without being born of water and Spirit," Jesus said. (John 3:5) What did Nicodemus want to know about the Spirit? The Spirit was like the wind, Jesus explained in one of the most wistful passages of Scripture, blowing where it chooses. One hears the sound of the wind without knowing where it comes from or where it is going. "So it is," he concludes, "with everyone who is born of the Spirit." (John 3:8) Birth, water and wind have one thing in common. They come to us. We have nothing to do with our own birth, and we do not make either water or wind. It is all a gift. Let the wind blow. Let it bring forth the water of life. Let the tank be filled. Let all the crud slip over the top and out. Let it happen, Nicodemus, let grace happen.

Let it happen in baptism. With water and the Spirit let God bring new life to the child. Let it happen every day thereafter with a simple "yes" to God. Let there be newness to each day so dramatic that it can only be described as a "new birth." Let there be a new center to life. Let there be a release from guilt through the forgiveness of sins. Let there be a new Spirit within us, filling us with power and purpose. Let there be the sparkling presence of faith, hope and love within us. Let God do it, Nicodemus, let grace happen.

And why can grace happen? Why can we expect to be filled by God? Because there is a power at loose in this world, a power called "God's Love." "For God so loved the world," Jesus explained, "that he gave his only Son, so that everyone who believes in him may not perish but may have eternal life." So begins the amazing story of what God has done in so many lives and what he can do in ours.

In her book, *Amazing Grace*, Kathleen Norris wrote about the renewing power of God's grace. She recalled the story of Jacob who had lied to his father and cheated his brother out of his rightful inheritance. Jacob sleeps and in his dream (Theophany) God finds him sleeping and would be well within his right to punish Jacob by taking his life at that vulnerable moment. Instead God gives Jacob a blessing. God saw not only what Jacob had done but also what he could become. Jacob awakens and praises God: "Surely the Lord is in this place—and I did not know it."

Norris also cited the examples of Peter and Saul (Paul), one having denied Jesus and the other having persecuted the early Christians. Again God saw not only what they had done but also what both of these men could become—the twin towers of early Christianity. That is what grace is all about. God accepts us even though we are unacceptable. God affirms us even though we deserve no affirmation. God finds us heading one way and turns us around to go a different direction. So our worship is a response to God's grace. We praise God, Norris wrote, not to observe our own faith but to give thanks for the faith God has placed in us.

David Bouchard wrote a delightful child's book called *If You're Not from the Prairie*, in which he claimed those who are not from the prairie do not and cannot know the sky, or the wind, or the sun, or the cold, or the meaning of flat. The book contains Bouchard's wonderful verse and also beautiful art by Henry Ripplinger. Here is a sampling.

> "If you're not from the prairie,
> You don't know the wind,
> You can't know the wind.
>
> Our cold winds of winter cut right to the core,
> Hot summer wind devils can blow down the door.
> As children we know when we play any game,
> The wind will be there, yet we play just the same.
>
> If you're not from the prairie,
> You don't know the wind."

Using Bouchard's format, may I speak of grace?

> If you're not God's child,
> You don't know grace.
> You can't know grace.
>
> Grace abounds as Jesus talks and walks with us,
> Grace fills each day and conquers every minus.
> To be forgiven is a gentle, summer rain,
> Making us fresh and new, like being born again.
>
> If you're not God's child
> You *don't* know grace.

Nicodemus may have hoped for a lesson in self improvement. Rather, he found himself in the presence of one who could fill his life with God. Instead of tickling his intellect with a new idea Jesus offered Nicodemus a new life. Did Nicodemus loosen the tightly secured handle and open the windmill of his soul so that it swung into the gusts of the Spirit? Did he let the water of life fill him? Or was he content to let the tank go dry and watch the moss spread slowly across the surface of his soul? Did he ever know grace?

OTHER TITLES BY THE AUTHOR:

Prairie Parables

A Road Once Traveled (and other Prairie Parables)

The Wild Rose and other Prairie Parables

*Additional copies of this or other books
by David Johnson can be obtained from:*

David Johnson
1701 Silver Creek Circle
Sioux Falls, SD 57106